PAUL AND HIS WORLD

Paul and His World

Stephen Tomkins

A LION BOOK

Reconstruction of King Herod's temple at the time of Paul. Detail from a model in the Holy Land Hotel, Jerusalem.

Previous page: St Paul the Apostle by Claude Vignon (1573–1670).

Page one: St Paul by the Master of the Pala Sforzesca (attrib.).

Copyright © 2004 Stephen Tomkins
This edition copyright © 2004 Lion Hudson

The author asserts the moral right
to be identified as the author of this work

A Lion Book
an imprint of
Lion Hudson plc
Mayfield House, 256 Banbury Road,
Oxford OX2 7DH, England
www.lionhudson.com
ISBN 0 7459 5129 5

First edition 2004
10 9 8 7 6 5 4 3 2 1 0

A catalogue record for this book is available
from the British Library

Typeset in 9/12 Modern 880
Printed and bound in China

Contents

Introduction

I t is paradoxical that the person who has had the most revolutionary impact on the shape and direction of Christianity since Jesus was not a reformer remaking an old and tired church centuries later, but an almost exact contemporary of Jesus. Of all Jesus' disciples, the one most influential in deciding how his faith would be handed on to future generations was the one who never knew him while he was alive. And the man who more than any other established Christianity as a world religion also spent years trying to wipe it off the face of the earth.

He has been revered as a Christian saint for 1,900 years, though many would say he has been more venerated than understood. However, he has become a highly suspect figure over the last 150 years for many theologians and for the general public, and even many Christians feel ambivalent about him. Some see him as a homophobic woman-hater. For some, he rewrote the Christian faith, turning Jesus from a Jewish teacher into a mythic crucified deity, his reinterpretation of Jesus eclipsing the original. Others say that his rejection of the law of Moses turned the church from a Jewish community into a persecutor of Jews. According to the *Jewish Encyclopedia*, he introduced an appallingly negative view of humankind into the faith: 'he robbed human life of its healthy impulses, the human soul of its faith in its own regenerating powers'. According to the philosopher Nietzsche, it was Paul's reinterpretation that crucified Jesus: 'The life, the example, the teaching, the death, the meaning and rule of the whole gospel – nothing was left once this hate-filled forger seized whatever he could use.'

By contrast, for many theologians of every camp and creed Paul is simply the greatest mind in Christian history. He understood Jesus better than anyone before or since and has communicated the mysteries of God like no other

Christian. Two thousand years later, we are still unravelling the complexities of his thinking, our eyes still adjusting to its brilliance. It would even be fair to say that many church traditions have given more weight to his words than Jesus'.

In fact Paul would be quite at home with such a mixed public – more at home thus than in stained glass. He had his share of hero worship in his lifetime, but was also more reviled than any other Christian. He was mobbed and stoned by non-Christian Jews as a blasphemer, imprisoned and scourged by Romans as a danger to society, scorned by Greek philosophers; and even many Christians abhorred him as a heretic. In the middle ground was the ambivalent majority, impressed by the heroic exploits and remarkable success of his mission to the Gentiles, but uncomfortable with his radicalism and divisiveness. He was called a bully and an approval seeker, a maverick apostate and a god, and – perhaps most shocking to later Christians – a rotten preacher.

What no one ever accused Paul of was being half-hearted. His Christian life was a constant, arduous missionary journey, enduring shipwrecks, prison, mob violence and the depressing politics of church life. He was unstoppable and unbreakable for one reason: 'this slight momentary affliction is preparing us for an eternal weight of glory beyond all measure'.

What we don't know about Paul could fill a library. His story is a fascinating one, but it is also frustratingly incomplete, and there is hardly a statement you could make about his life that has not been contradicted by one expert or another. Did he preach to Jews? Was he a Roman citizen? Did he convert to Christianity? Did he have a vision on the road to Damascus? Was he executed? Which of the letters in the Bible did he write? Did he believe Christ was God? Was he educated in Jerusalem? We do not even know what his full name was – or do we?

Paul did biographers the favour of writing letters, and somewhere between seven and thirteen have survived, so we do have plenty of unquestionable information about his teachings. This is more than you can say for anyone else in the New Testament: the authorship of all the other letters has often been questioned – and robustly defended in response – and arguments about how much of the Gospels (and which bits) offer reliable indications of what Jesus said continue unresolvably. Paul's letters give us only scattered details about his travels, friends and the story of his life. The book of Acts tells us a great deal about Paul's mission, but scholars are very divided about how reliable it is: from historically faultless to more or less useless. And even if we accept it implicitly, it leaves vast and important blanks in Paul's life.

I cannot help comparing this with John Wesley, whose biography I have also written. He left thousands of letters, along with a twenty-four-volume *Journal* and shelf-loads of other writings, yet certain parts of his life are still fogged in mystery. What hope then of knowing Paul?

My own interpretation is that we have a lot of reliable information about Paul, but very little certainty. As a result, there are a lot of 'probablies', 'maybes' and 'it seemses' in this book, which is unfortunate as they can sometimes get in the way of a good story. Other writers on Paul have chosen to smooth over the 'probablies' and, having decided which version of events to adopt, then presented that version as if it were the only one. This is entirely reasonable and reads well, but for me, with a story so veiled in uncertainty as Paul's, honesty insists that best guesses and suppositions are not presented as fact. Or if not insists, at least requests, for if one followed that policy in every instance the book would be unreadable, so even here there are many statements that should be read as questions.

There are various attitudes one can take to the New Testament as a source of information. Some Christians would maintain that, since it is the word of God, every statement it makes is infallibly, historically accurate – a claim the Bible never makes for itself. Conversely, the most sceptical scholars would say that its stories, being full of miracles and religious propaganda, are completely unreliable as fact. In the present book, I am looking at the New Testament as a historical source, asking – as you would any other source – how close the writers were to events, how consistent they are, what bias they show, etc., and then following the evidence wherever it leads. The New Testament emerges from this test as a reliable and useful account of Paul and the early church.

Our picture of Paul will always be patchy, like a faded icon or a disintegrating parchment. And even when we see clearly there is no guarantee that we have understood. Nevertheless, we can try. Two thousand million people today are followers of Jesus, and every one of them sees him through a lens crafted by Paul. A person of that influence is worth getting to know.

Paul's Worlds

P aul was born into two different worlds. He was a Jew in a Roman culture, a Roman citizen in a separatist Jewish church. He even had two names: to fellow Jews he was *Sha'ul*, Saul, after the first king of Israel who was from his own tribe of Benjamin; to the wider world he was known by his threefold Latin name, the only part of which we know is *Paulus*, Paul. (The idea that he changed his name on conversion is a popular misconception based on the fact that the book of Acts calls him Saul when he is among Jews and then Paul when he is out in the Roman world.)

These two worlds were in an uneasy truce. Their contrasting cultures and the tensions between them form the background that shaped and will help us make sense of Paul's tumultuous life.

The Roman world

There have been few better times in history for the spread of new ideas than the first two centuries AD. The Roman empire was at its full extent, encompassing the entire Mediterranean world and more. The civil wars that had engulfed Rome for decades were ended by the victory of Caesar Augustus, leaving most of the known world not only in peace but also politically and culturally unified. Paul could address Romans, Greeks, Palestinian Jews, Syrians, Arabians, Cypriots, Maltese and inhabitants of what are now Turkey and the Balkans, all in one language, and not until the nineteenth century could he have travelled between them faster.

The culture of the Roman empire was, paradoxical though it seems, largely Greek, at least in the eastern half. Language, literature and thought were Greek, and so were the gods.

'The various modes of worship which prevailed in the Roman world were all considered by the people as equally true, and by the philosophers as equally false, and by the magistrates as equally useful.'

EDWARD GIBBON

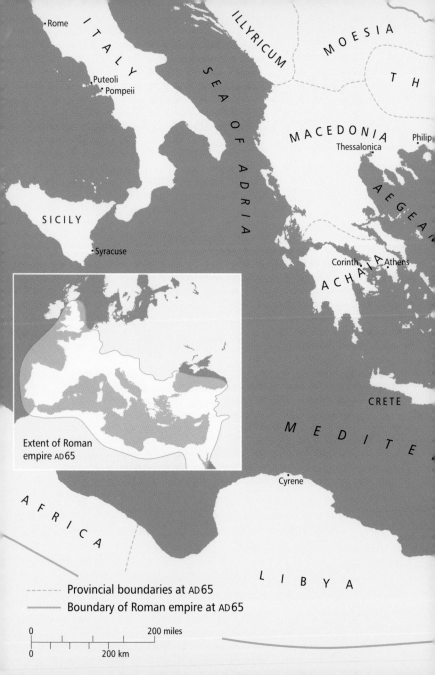

Rome

ITALY

Puteoli
Pompeii

SICILY

Syracuse

ILLYRICUM

MOESIA

SEA OF ADRIA

MACEDONIA

Thessalonica

Philip

AEGEAN

Corinth   Athens

ACHAIA

CRETE

MEDITER

Extent of Roman
empire AD 65

Cyrene

AFRICA

LIBYA

- - - - - Provincial boundaries at AD 65
─────── Boundary of Roman empire at AD 65

| 0 | | | | 200 miles |
| 0 | | | | 200 km |

EUXINE SEA

CE

Heraclea

BITHYNIA AND PONTUS

MYSIA

ASIA

Pergamum

LYDIA

Smyrna

Sardis

Ephesus

Miletus

CARIA

Laodicea

Colossae

PHRYGIA

Antioch

PISIDIA

LYCIA

PAMPHYLIA

Ancyra

GALATIA

Iconium

CAPPADOCIA

CILICIA

Tarsus

CYPRUS

MEDITERRANEAN SEA

EA

ANEAN SEA

Antioch

SYRIA

PHOENICIA

Damascus

Tyre

Caesarea

JUDEA

Jerusalem

Alexandria

EGYPT

NABATEAN KINGDOM

Petra

ARABIA

*'Wars have so far
vanished they
are considered
historical
legends. A man
can travel from
one country
to another as if
it were his
native land.'*

AELIUS ARISTIDES,
C. 150

Traditional religion in the Roman world was something we might barely recognize as religion: it occupied a different part of life. The gods were spirits with responsibility for one's family and city, in control of the weather and the fertility of crops and of women, and offering success in love, war and business. The role of the priests has been filled in modern life not so much by the clergy as by economists, meteorologists and pesticides. Prayer and sacrifice were offered by the community en masse, led by its patriarchs, as an attempt to secure prosperity. 'Atheism' – which is what Jews and Christians were accused of when they refused to sacrifice – was not so much heretical as anti-social.

And yet, paganism was intrinsically tolerant. The Romans had little reason to stop subject peoples appeasing their local deities, as long as they sacrificed to the gods of Rome too. Moreover, as Roman gods were clearly powerful figures worth getting on the right side of, subjects were generally happy to do so.

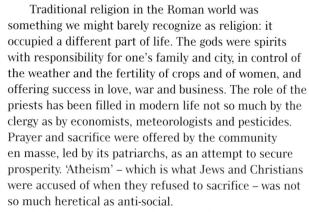

But traditional religion lacked much that we would consider essential to religion: moral teaching, transcendent awe, spiritual growth, relationship with God and personal salvation. As a result, many turned to 'mystery religions', which were more personal and exciting, such as the Persian cult of Mithras where initiates showered in bulls' blood.

The god Mithras, depicted as usual killing a bull, his most celebrated exploit. A second-century marble relief.

The Jewish world
Judaism was a significant feature on the religious landscape of the empire. In Paul's day there were, as now, more Jews outside Palestine than inside. Displaced by war, or encouraged to seek their fortune in new settlements, they had established Jewish communities throughout the empire, concentrated mainly in the large cities of the East and in Rome. Alexandria (in Egypt), the largest city in the

empire after Rome, was perhaps one-third Jewish.

Judaism had a mixed public image. Its worship of one sovereign God had a credibility among educated people that the pagan panoply of celestial superheroes lacked. So too did its ancient scriptures, earthy realistic spirituality, high moral standards, community life and – locally – its focus on prayer and praise rather than animal sacrifice. And yet these very things also created suspicion and resentment: devotion to one God excluded Jews from doing their bit to gain the gods' favour; abhorrence of pagan ritual kept them out of the army and public service;

and they often shunned local social life on moral grounds. Circumcision seemed simply barbaric.

So on the one hand, a significant number of non-Jews converted to the faith and became 'God-fearers' (though only a minority went all the way and got circumcised and followed the Torah, the law of Moses). On the other hand, Jews were widely distrusted as an arrogant, aloof and unpatriotic subculture. In times of political unrest they could face violence, but being a highly productive seven

Jesus in conflict with Pharisees over the woman caught in adultery. *Christ and the Adultress* by Rocco Marconi, sixteenth century.

per cent of the empire they were officially licensed to dissent from Roman religion.

Then, as now, there were varieties of Judaism. For a start there was a divide between the dispersion and the homeland. It was easy for the Jews of the dispersion, living in a Greek culture, with even their prayers and scriptures in Greek, and distanced from the religion of the temple, to absorb Greek ways and ideas. Equally, though, it could have the opposite effect, and, deprived of the temple, they could turn more militant in their devotion to

The philosophers

The moral high ground in the Roman world was occupied not by religion but by philosophy, which far from being an indulgence in abstract conundrums was concerned above all with the right way to live. The most popular in the first century was Stoicism, which saw the world as inanimate matter given shape, life and harmony by logos, the divine reason that is manifested both in the human soul and in the gods. Living a life of reason and virtue in accord with logos is the only true happiness, because finding pleasure in anything in the outside world makes one a slave to changing circumstances.

Platonism was equally austere and ascetic, considering the body an unwanted cage for the rational soul and the material world a mere shadow of the eternal. Unlike Stoicism it did at least offer the immortality of the soul.

Epicureans believed the universe was an accident, untouched by the gods, and that pleasure is the ultimate good. However, pleasure was best achieved through self-denial and contemplation.

But philosophy was, like medieval monasticism, a path for a heroic élite only. Ordinary people took their hats off to it and carried on life as normal.

A bust of the Greek philosopher Plato.

the law of Moses than their fellows in Jerusalem.

Such questions of compromise and fidelity fuelled the movements within Judaism. Sadduceeism was the religion of Jerusalem's priestly ruling class, less than fanatical in their religious observance and in favour of anything that promoted social stability and good relations with Rome.

At the opposite pole was Paul's party, the Pharisees. They pursued purity through a meticulous observation of not only the law of Moses, but also the strict traditions of the scribes, the interpreters of Moses. (This was the main issue over which they clashed with Jesus.) Like the Greek philosophers, they were too demanding to become a mass movement, but were widely admired by ordinary believers, whom they encouraged to greater purity. Naturally unhappy to be ruled by godless, demon-worshipping Romans, Pharisees were sometimes involved in armed resistance.

What about the faith of the vast majority of ordinary Jews? They lived, with greater or lesser thoroughness, by the law of Moses – which has often been seen by Christians as a matter of petty legalism, but this is an unjustifiable caricature. They worshipped and heard the scriptures at the local synagogue each week (which was also a social and administrative centre), and would aim to visit the temple somewhere between three times a year and once in a lifetime, depending on proximity and enthusiasm. Above all, they knew themselves to be the chosen people of God. They had been delivered from slavery and established as a nation, but were now under intolerable oppression from the godless, and – some would say – shamefully compromised themselves.

Consequently, they lived with the overwhelming expectation that God would again intervene to deliver, vindicate and purify them.

CHAPTER 2

'My Earlier Life in Judaism'

P aul was born at around the same time as Jesus, but in Tarsus in Asia Minor (modern Turkey) rather than in the Palestinian countryside. Tarsus was a large, flourishing city near the Mediterranean coast, on the Roman road that led north through the formidable Taurus mountains and east into Syria. It was the capital of the Roman province of Cilicia.

Paul's family were devout Jews, who among themselves seem to have spoken Aramaic, the language of the motherland, as well as Greek. As Pharisees, they brought Paul up to know the scriptures and follow the interpretations of the scribes. But the family were also Roman citizens and citizens of Tarsus, which granted them various legal privileges as well as social standing. A traditional story has Paul's parents being taken to Tarsus from Palestine as prisoners of war, becoming citizens on release from slavery.

Not surprisingly, the family maintained links with the homeland, and sent Paul to school in Jerusalem. A gifted and fervent scholar, he studied as a young man under Gamaliel, the greatest rabbi of the time and a leader of the Pharisees. Acts has Paul tell the Jerusalem mob, 'I am a Jew, born in Tarsus in Cilicia, but brought up in this city at the feet of Gamaliel, educated strictly according to our ancestral law, being zealous for God as you are.'

Already, however, we are on controversial ground: most of this information so far is from the book of Acts, and many New Testament experts have grave reservations about its historical accuracy, denying that Paul was either a Roman citizen or educated in Jerusalem. Paul makes no mention of his impressive schooling in passages where he cites his Jewish credentials; neither does he ever use his threefold Roman name. Arguments from silence, however, are notoriously unreliable, and when the whole story of the latter part of Acts turns upon Paul's citizenship, we need more than silence from Paul to make such information incredible. Again, Paul says,

The book of Acts

Paul's letters offer only brief glimpses into his life story, so most of our information comes from Acts. Acts is the sequel to Luke's Gospel, telling the stories of the first church and of Paul from before his conversion until his imprisonment in Rome.

But how reliable is Acts? Many scholars distrust it. On the one hand, it sometimes conflicts with information, or at least impressions, given in Paul's letters. The theology of Paul's sermons in Acts is generically Christian rather than distinctly Paul's. It is full of miracles, and it portrays the church more harmoniously than Paul does. (Likewise, in Luke's Gospel, when drawing from Mark, he consistently edits out information that reflects too harshly on the apostles.) Acts takes pains to blame non-Christian Jews for their schism with Christians and seems rather biased against them. It is usually dated AD 80–90, two decades after Paul's death.

On the other hand, there are passages in the first person, suggesting the writer knew Paul personally, and Acts ends most inconclusively, as if it had simply brought the story up to date so far. Such firsthand knowledge may be very hard to accept, but all other explanations offered are equally problematic. The extreme scepticism of many scholars about Luke's knowledge of Paul, just decades (at most) after the events, is overdone, and might profitably be applied to their own ability to reconstruct his life 2,000 years later, in defiance of Acts, from between the lines of half a dozen letters.

Acts is the only window we have into most of Paul's life, though frosted and perhaps rose-tinted, so it is an invaluable source of information.

'Three times I was beaten with rods,' a punishment that a Roman citizen should not have been subjected to. There is, however, a difference between 'should not' and 'would not', and the author of Acts was well aware that it had happened to Paul.

Paul writes – or dictates – Greek confidently and naturally, but without any trace of a serious classical education. Rather, his letters are steeped in the scriptures and the interpretative techniques of the rabbis. This is precisely what one would expect of a man who has lived at large in the Greco-Roman world, but been schooled in the Jewish subculture, reflecting Luke's information rather well. Paul's birth in Tarsus is also mentioned only in Acts, but even the most sceptical New Testament scholars choose to accept this wholeheartedly.

The picture we get of Paul's first two or three decades, therefore, is of a life divided between the Jewish communities of the dispersion and the homeland,

The Expulsion of the Money-changers from the Temple. Fourteenth-century Macedonian fresco.

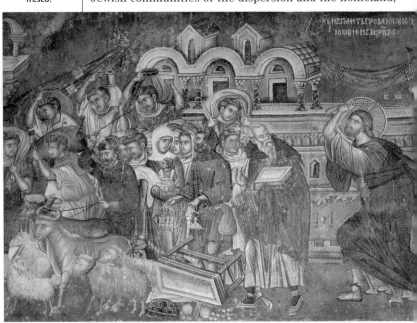

though how the time was divided between the two is impossible to say.

It is not clear precisely what Paul did for a living, but apparently like Jesus he was a skilled manual labourer. His own account is merely that he grew weary from the work of his hands. Acts tells us that he was a *skenopoios*, which is usually translated 'tentmaker', but it could equally mean 'leatherworker'. The majority of tents were made from leather anyway, but they were sometimes made from a goathair cloth from Paul's home in Cilicia, so that instead may have been his medium.

This trade would by no means have precluded Paul from being a religious teacher, as – in later times at least – rabbis were expected to work. Whether he was one or not, we have no indication. It has even been argued that Paul was a Pharisee missionary to the Gentiles, an intriguing speculation with no solid evidence to support it.

'He saw Paul coming, a man small in size, bald-headed, bandy-legged, well-built, with eyebrows meeting, rather long-nosed, full of grace.'

THE ACTS OF PAUL
AND THECLA,
SECOND CENTURY

Paul and Jesus

At some point, Paul came across Jesus of Nazareth, though whether during his lifetime we do not know. It is quite possible that Paul was in Jerusalem for Passover in the last week of Jesus' life (probably in April AD 30). Jesus was given a messiah's welcome, ran riot in the temple and occupied it, and engaged in public conflict with every religious party, causing enough disturbance to get him arrested and publicly executed.

The image of Paul the anonymous Pharisee standing seething in the crowd around the presumptuous Nazarene is captivating, though of course purely speculative. Paul does say, 'Even though we once knew Christ according to the flesh, we know him no longer in that way,' conceivably referring to an acquaintance during his life – but his main point here is simply that he once saw Christ through human eyes alone and now sees the truth as revealed by God.

When Jesus was killed, his followers, discredited and endangered by his disgrace, disappeared from public view.

Doubtless many Jews were disappointed, while others thought he had got what he deserved, but everybody knew his story was over.

However, the next time the people descended on Jerusalem, for the feast of Pentecost seven weeks later, Jesus' followers were back in the limelight, proclaiming that he had risen bodily from the dead. According to Acts, the resurrected Jesus having spent most of the intervening time privately teaching them and then having been taken up to heaven, the 120 disciples were suddenly filled with God's Spirit and preached the resurrection in miraculously given foreign languages.

This story reflects the fact that from the very start the Christians were missionaries, publicly proclaiming and spreading their faith in Jerusalem. And so, one way or another, sooner or later, Paul gave ear to the gospel of Jesus. He did not like it.

The Holy Spirit comes upon the apostles on the day of Pentecost. A seventeenth-century painting by El Greco.

The First Church

Whatat was this first church like? To start with the obvious but crucial answer, it was Jewish, and not just racially but religiously. In no sense did the first Christians see themselves as preaching a new religion. They believed Jesus was the long-awaited messiah of Israel, sent by God to restore Judaism where it was awry and to bring it to a new level of fulfilment. Consequently, they continued to worship in the temple, observe the sabbath and study the scriptures.

The central point of Jesus' teaching had been the kingdom of God: he declared that God's rule was breaking into the world in a new way through him, and he invited his hearers to become part of it by joining the community of his followers and living renewed lives. Now the Christians naturally continued to preach this kingdom, but with a new emphasis. If the death of Jesus had seemed to disprove his claims and teaching, his resurrection turned the tables, being God's seal of approval and proving his message true. It also made it clear that he was a unique individual whom everyone that wanted to know God would have to come to terms with. So, above all, Christians preached the resurrection of the messiah. Instead of just continuing to proclaim the message of Jesus, they proclaimed Jesus.

Acts tells us that they held public meetings in the temple, in Solomon's portico. They also met in private, where they learned from their teachers, the apostles. These were more than the 'twelve disciples' of Jesus. In 1 Corinthians 15:5–7, a passage that almost certainly quotes an earlier creed, Paul writes, 'He appeared to Cephas [Peter], then to the twelve... Then he appeared to James, then to all the apostles,' characteristically

'Being fully assured by the resurrection of our Lord Jesus Christ... they went forth proclaiming that the kingdom of God was at hand.'

CLEMENT OF ROME, C. 96

The Resurrection of Christ, from *Scenes from the Life of Christ*, painted by the fourteenth-century Bohemian Master of Hohenfurth.

distinguishing between the 'apostles' as a whole and 'the twelve'. 'Apostles', literally meaning 'the sent', was a rare word for 'messengers', and denotes all those who had met the resurrected Jesus and been commissioned by him to preach his message. At the start, they must have been more or less the whole church.

The twelve were their leaders. Jesus had evidently liked the symbolism of having twelve close disciples, reflecting the twelve patriarchs of a renewed Israel – although judging from the lists of names in the Gospels they may not have always been the same twelve throughout his mission. According to the Gospels, even from among the twelve, Jesus chose an inner circle of Peter and the brothers James and John, all Galilean fishermen. This seems to have continued now, with Peter taking the overall lead.

Into this potentially quite tidy pyramid, comes the more awkward figure of James, Jesus' brother. The Gospels agree that he did not accept or approve of Jesus while he was alive, but Paul mentions him as one of those to whom the risen Lord appeared. By the start of Acts he has quietly joined the followers, but has no part to play until after Paul's conversion when he suddenly appears to be the leader of the Jerusalem church. Paul names him as an 'acknowledged pillar' of the church. What kind of road-to-Damascus experience turned James around we have no idea, nor when it happened. He was known as James the Righteous, reflecting a devotion to the Torah; and while this devotion may be what caused his earlier rejection of Jesus, it was not abandoned when he became a follower. James's Christian spirituality was seriously different from Paul's, bringing some creative conflict to the New Testament. His prominence is reflected in the fact that he is the only Christian to be mentioned in any non-Christian writing in the first century.

Food and water: the Lord's supper and baptism

As well as teaching and prayer, when the Christians were together they placed great importance on sharing food and wine. What is not clear is to what extent this was the familiar Holy Communion service, where they saw in bread and wine the body and blood of the crucified messiah, and to what extent it was simply communal dining. Paul's instructions to the Corinthians twenty years later most emphatically take the former line, though still in the context of a full meal. The synoptic Gospels later still offered the same interpretation in their record of the last supper. Moreover, Paul's comments address the practice of what sounds like a longstanding tradition at the heart of Christian worship. His summary of it is close enough to the Gospel accounts to suggest that it had already long been formalized, and was therefore of very early origin. And yet, by contrast, all Acts ever says, from these early days through to

'He [James] drank neither wine nor strong drink, ate no flesh, never shaved or anointed himself with ointment or bathed... He... went alone into the temple and prayed on behalf of the people, insomuch that his knees were reputed to have acquired the hardness of camels' knees.'

HEGESIPPUS,
SECOND CENTURY,
ON JAMES

Paul's last years, is 'They broke bread,' which could refer to such a service or merely to their eating together. What is more, as late as about AD 100, a church manual known as the *Didache* provides a liturgy for the Eucharist that, staggeringly, completely fails to mention the death, body or blood of Jesus, being closer to Jewish daily mealtime grace. It seems that both body-and-blood and mere communal eating traditions existed side by side in the church until the latter version of the meal eventually swallowed the former.

Many, especially among the leaders, were not permanent residents in Jerusalem, or had not been until now. But then they had not been permanent residents anywhere very much since they had been following Jesus. They had toured the Palestinian countryside with him, and he had sent many of them off travelling in pairs to preach the gospel. They could have expected to be sheltered and fed, as it was a tradition of Jewish culture to give hospitality to preachers.

'The early Christians... enjoyed the inestimable advantage of believing that the millennium was near, which precluded them from seeking to establish a beneficent regime in this world.'

MALCOLM
MUGGERIDGE

One would assume, then, that with Christianity now largely transplanted to Jerusalem, the Galilean veterans were accommodated by those who had houses in Jerusalem, or found places to share. If so, Luke's repeated assertion that the believers 'were together and had all things in common' makes a good deal of sense, not so much as an ideological experiment in communism (though there were precedents for that in first-century Judaism), but as a way of providing for the influx. The church was already not short of old ladies, and so a daily distribution of food was arranged for widows – such as, one might suppose, Jesus' mother, who is mentioned in Acts as a member of the church.

However, not all Christians were now in Jerusalem. The story of Luke–Acts is profoundly shaped by the author's sense of the progress of Christianity from Galilee to Jerusalem in Luke and from Jerusalem to Rome in Acts, so he now focuses on the main church in Jerusalem, ignoring whatever may have been happening elsewhere, just as for the second half of the book he focuses on Paul's travels to the exclusion of all other Christian leaders. Doubtless pockets of believers in Jesus remained throughout the north country.

An intriguing aspect of the life of the first church, closely linked by both Paul and Acts with baptism, is the gift of the Holy Spirit. Jewish scriptures used 'the spirit' as a way of talking about God's activity in the world, empowering the prophets to bring his word, and directing the moral life of Israel; and the coming of the messiah was expected to bring a wider visitation of God's spirit. Both Paul and Acts expect everyone baptized into

The Preaching of St Peter, fourteenth century.

the church to receive the Holy Spirit, and Acts also reflects Paul's ideas about what difference this makes: he brings miraculous powers and messages from God, and inspires the community's worship and mission.

On the role of women in this church, Acts has little to say, other than noting that they joined the men in prayer. The Gospels make it abundantly clear that Jesus had many female disciples – demonstrating an unusually progressive attitude – and Paul's letters show that (whatever his attitude may have been to women's teaching) they continued to be disciples in his churches. Offering a small hint of something more, the Pentecost story in Acts has the 120 men and women all together in one place when the Spirit comes on each one of them and 'all of them were filled with the Holy Spirit and began to speak in other languages', proclaiming God's deeds of power. The fact that Luke immediately links this to a scripture about both sons and daughters prophesying, and slaves, both men and women, receiving the Spirit, suggests that he may believe women would have been preaching alongside the men – though of course this is reading somewhat between the lines.

Baptism in the first church

Those who joined the Christians were initiated by being baptized in water in the name of Jesus. Acts mentions this repeatedly, and Paul's letters assume that all Christians have been baptized into Christ. Oddly, the synoptic Gospels never once mention Jesus or his followers baptizing (although the Gospel of John does twice).

Baptism had long been used to initiate Gentile believers into Judaism, and John the Baptist had more recently courted controversy by claiming that Jews themselves needed to be baptized in repentance for their sins. John's movement and Jesus' were closely linked, so Christians presumably inherited baptism from John, but came to interpret it as bringing mystical union with Christ as well as symbolizing repentance.

The language barrier

One last aspect of the church in these first few years is a major cultural divide between the Greek-speaking Jews of the dispersion and the Aramaic-speaking natives. This is something we know of only from Acts, but which many modern scholars not only accept, but also make much more of than Luke does himself – and convincingly so.

Luke does not even mention the divide until Acts 6 when it becomes necessary as background to the story of Stephen. He has, after all, been stressing the unity of the believers. And all he says now is that the Greek-speakers or 'Hellenists' complained that their widows were being overlooked in the apostolic meals on wheels, and so the twelve arranged for 'seven men of good standing, full of the Spirit and wisdom' to take on the task while they concentrated on prayer and preaching. (This has traditionally been understood as the founding of the office of deacon, which literally means 'servant', but Acts does not make this connection.)

The first oddity of Luke's story is that all seven have Greek names (while naturally the twelve almost all have Hebrew names). The second is that all the stories that Luke then recounts of the seven are about them preaching

and performing miracles – i.e. acting like the twelve themselves, instead of doing the menial work that was supposed to release the twelve to do it. It looks very much as if the division of labour between the seven and the twelve was not so much between pastoral administration and preaching as between

Detail from a fourth-century sarcophagus showing the baptism of Cornelius by Peter.

the two communities, Aramaic-speaking and Greek-speaking, each group doing the same jobs for its respective community.

Could it be that this was the real role of the seven? It makes a lot of sense, not just of the information here but of what is to come later, and in fact Acts itself is quite patient of this interpretation. Reading Acts in this light, the twelve are trying to oversee the ever-growing numbers of Christians in Jerusalem, teaching, distributing food, etc. Owing to the language/cultural barrier, many Hellenists are getting missed out; but when this is pointed out it looks as if this pastoral work could be in danger of swallowing up their whole time. So seven Hellenists are appointed to organize provision for (and to teach) their own group, allowing the twelve to devote enough of their time to preaching the word (while still doing pastoral work for the Aramaic community).

Though somewhat speculative, this is at least a reconstruction that does justice to both the concrete information in Acts and the implication beneath its surface of a culturally divided community. It is important to do so, because this division also seems to have played a crucial part in the violent assaults against the church that now came.

The First Assault

Paul's letters confirm Acts' story that, before his conversion, as a zealous Pharisee, he attacked the Christian community and tried to destroy it. What Acts alone tells us is, firstly, that before this Pharisaic assault the Christians were more than once attacked by the Sadducees, the priestly ruling party of Jerusalem, and secondly, that in this earlier period the Christians were very popular among the ordinary people of the city.

Sadducees versus Christians

That the Sadducees should have been ahead of the Pharisees in such an offensive is not in the least surprising, as they were the more natural enemies of Christianity. It is ironic that 'the Pharisees and Sadducees' tend to get lumped together by Bible-readers as indistinguishable opponents of Jesus: it is as if Muslims of the future were to look back and refer to twentieth-century opponents of Islam as 'the communists and capitalists'. The Pharisees had a great deal in common with Christians, both of them being fervently committed to living out the Jewish faith in day-to-day life without compromise and regardless of personal cost, and both having a passion for the coming of the kingdom of God. Jesus' clashes with them came because on the one hand they disliked his laxity about ritual purity, and because he, on the other hand, considered their passion for purity to lack compassion for people and to slide into double standards and legalism – and precisely because they otherwise trod much of the same ground.

The Sadducees, in contrast, represented the religion of the status quo, of moneyed interest and of staying on the right side of Rome. They consisted entirely of the temple priesthood, and were closely attached to Herod, the hated puppet king of the Romans. They denied the existence of spirits and the resurrection of the dead and accepted only the five books of Moses as scripture: in all this the Pharisees and Christians were as one against them. Probably the reason why, in the Gospels, Jesus clashes so much more with the Pharisees is simply that he barely encounters the Sadducees before he comes to Jerusalem.

Why should the Sadducees so want to stamp out

John the Baptist preaches before King Herod and Queen Herodias. Thirteenth-century mosaic from the Baptistry, Florence, depicting scenes from the life of John the Baptist.

Christianity? Above all, because it was a messianic movement. The messiah was generally expected to be a revolutionary leader, overthrowing Roman rule and the Herodian monarchy, and either reigning himself or making way for the unmediated reign of God. No one whose rule was tied up with the Romans and Herod could afford to tolerate such a movement. Once Jesus had ridden into Jerusalem, had been proclaimed king by the crowds and then had assaulted their temple,

the Sadducees saw how dangerous he was.

He himself had now been disposed of, but if his followers were still preaching the kingdom of God after his death, they could be expected to continue his revolutionary plans. The fact that the person that the high priests had had executed was now being proclaimed as God's right-hand man in heaven cannot have helped matters. Acts has Peter telling them that his healing of a disabled man was achieved 'in the name of Jesus the Messiah of Nazareth, whom you crucified, whom God raised from the dead'; and one can see that this would not incline them to smile on Christianity indulgently.

What was more, Christianity had now become focused on resurrection. The Sadducees did not deny the resurrection of the dead out of mere scepticism, but because it was closely associated with revolution. Not only was the resurrection of Israel a metaphor for its liberation from Rome, but also a literal resurrection of the dead was promised in the coming kingdom; and this promise was an enticement to revolutionaries to lay down their lives in the cause. If, as seems likely, the first Christians proclaimed the resurrection of Jesus, like Paul did later, as the 'first fruits' of a general resurrection, then the movement must have seemed in many ways a greater threat than ever since his death.

According to Acts, first Peter and John, and then a larger group of the apostles, were arrested by the authorities for preaching this message in the temple, but both times they were freed. The first release was because they were so popular among the people that priestly hands were tied. The second was because of the moderating influence on the Jerusalem council of Gamaliel, the leader of the Pharisees.

This brings us round to the other side of Acts' story of the first church: its great popularity. Luke repeatedly reports not only that their teachers preached to vast crowds and that their numbers swelled remarkably, but also that the Christians enjoyed the good will of the people.

This is something that has no confirmation outside the first five chapters of Acts, but it is worth asking what would account for such popularity, if true. Luke points mainly to the miracles performed by the apostles; and the spectacle it presents of their standing up to the rulers who try to silence them is also impressive. We can add to this the fact that the claims of Jesus' resurrection must have been taken thoroughly seriously by a lot of people, not just the Christians. This would seem highly unlikely to us in the sceptical modern world, but remember that resurrection was a popular belief – expectation even – among first-century Jews. They were waiting for a general resurrection rather than for one man to rise from the dead, but with such an outlook they would be far more open to the preaching of the Christians than we might assume. In fact, bearing in mind the conflict between the Pharisees and Sadducees over this belief, one can imagine Christian preaching of the resurrection positively endearing them to the Pharisees and their supporters. Another thing that such popularity would suggest about the Christians is that they were seen to live by the law of Moses – despite the rather different attitude that became prominent later.

The scattering of the church

Nothing of what we have seen so far prepares us for the onslaught that the Christians then suddenly faced. According to Acts, Stephen, one of the seven, provoked opposition by his preaching and was arrested for blasphemy and stoned to death; and then the church was engulfed by a wave of violence which dispersed it throughout Palestine.

This story in Acts is an immediate continuation from that slightly puzzling election of the seven, and it continues to puzzle. Apart from the question of how Christianity could suddenly become so hated, the main problem is that Luke tells us that though the whole church was put to flight, its leaders stayed in Jerusalem with impunity: 'A severe persecution began against the

'The more we are mown down by you, the more we grow. The blood of Christians is seed.'

TERTULLIAN,
SECOND CENTURY

*The Martyrdom
of St Stephen*,
engraved by
Gustave Doré,
1866.

church in Jerusalem, and all except the apostles were
scattered throughout the countryside of Judea and
Samaria.' Is it not against all reason and experience that
those who want to destroy a movement should go to the
trouble of attacking its entire membership, while letting
its leadership carry on untouched? Surely one strikes the
shepherds and the sheep are scattered.

The clue to what is happening here may be that all
those whom Acts mentions specifically as being dispersed
from Jerusalem seem to be Christians from the Jewish
dispersion, the Hellenists: Philip, one of the seven; and
'men of Cyprus and Cyrene'. Because of this, many

scholars argue that it was the Greek-speaking church that was attacked, not the whole church, allowing the native believers and apostles to remain in Jerusalem unmolested.

Why would the church's enemies make such a discrimination in their offensive? Presumably because the different Christian groups not only spoke different languages, but also had some different beliefs or practices. The accusation against Stephen, Acts says, was that 'This man never stops saying things against the holy place and the Law; for we have heard him say that this Jesus of Nazareth will destroy this place and will change the customs that Moses handed on to us.' Luke assures us the charge was false – but how false? Presumably it reflects something about Stephen's conduct and teaching that the people of Jerusalem objected to. We have very good evidence that Jesus predicted the destruction of the temple, and one charge at his own trial was that he had said, 'I will destroy this temple that is made with hands, and in three days I will build another, not made with hands.' According to John's Gospel, Jesus had indeed said something along these lines, but should be understood metaphorically, the 'temple' being himself. Add to this the fact that the writers of the New Testament agree in interpreting Jesus' death as a sacrifice for sins (sacrifice being the main function of the temple), and one cannot but wonder whether Stephen and his friends might have started to believe that in some sense the messiah had superseded the temple. Perhaps they started to argue that Jesus' sacrificial death had made the temple sacrifices less important, or even redundant. Perhaps they claimed that, now believers had God's Spirit within them, they were, in Paul's words, 'temples of the Holy Spirit', finding the Lord as immediately present with them as he was said to be in the inner sanctum of the temple. If so, one can see why it was those Christians who had spent their lives in the Greek world, far from the temple, who took to such ideas more readily than their Palestinian counterparts.

If they did teach that temple sacrifices were

redundant, this would also account for the charge of changing the customs that Moses handed on, as sacrifice was a central part of the law of Moses. It is equally possible that the Hellenist Christians caused offence with their laxity with regard to other laws of Moses: Jesus had spoken controversially about both sabbath and food laws, for example. All this requires a certain amount of supposition, but it is accepted by many scholars and does at least illustrate the kind of developments in Christianity that might have antagonized fellow Jews.

If this modern interpretation of Acts is right, then there was a significant cultural divide in the Jerusalem church in its first few years, between the Aramaic-speaking majority and the Greek-speaking minority, which the writer of Acts is not disposed to focus upon. Separate leaders were elected for the latter, and their Christianity rapidly developed in a more controversial direction. The first wave of anti-Christian attacks was against them, rather than the church as a whole, allowing the Aramaic church and its apostles to remain in Jerusalem unharmed.

However, this is not the only reasonable understanding of what happened in the first anti-Christian campaign, and there are problems with it. It is intrinsically unlikely that Jerusalem should turn with such bloody violence against the Christian message of the Hellenists but continue to give the Aramaic-speaking Christians the benefit of the doubt. Surely 'Death to the Christians' is a more likely rallying cry than 'Death to the Greek-speaking Christians'. Moreover, when Paul's letters mention his attack, they never differentiate between Hellenists and Hebrews, merely saying that he 'persecuted the church'.

So if we are to question Acts' statement that the whole church was scattered but the apostles remained, we could equally come to the reverse conclusion: that both Aramaic- and Greek-speakers were indeed scattered, and that this included the apostles. After all, those stories following the death of Stephen in Acts that involve any of the twelve all take place outside Jerusalem – Peter and

John visiting Philip in Samaria and preaching throughout the region, Peter going 'here and there among all the believers', visiting Lydda and staying in Joppa.

Acts' statement about the apostles remaining in Jerusalem is the only evidence we have that the attacks discriminated between the two Christian communities. But it could be that Luke makes the statement merely as a way of preparing for what follows next – the story of Philip in Samaria, which involves Peter and John being sent there from Jerusalem, where they return afterwards. However, the fact that these two travel from Jerusalem does not mean that the whole leadership must have remained permanently in Jerusalem throughout the troubles.

Perhaps then the best interpretation of the information in Acts is, as usual, an untidier one: that the Greek-speaking church first provoked the anti-Christian backlash and, though it affected all Christians, they suffered the worst of it; that, since Jerusalem was becoming a dangerous place, many Christians – especially the Hellenists, but also the Aramaic-speakers, including the apostles – took to missionary travels around the country, without all being permanently exiled from the city; but that at the same time a Christian presence – and an apostolic one – remained in Jerusalem, despite the coming and going of individuals.

One thing we can be sure of: for those who wanted to see Christianity eradicated, the campaign was a monumental disaster, spreading the teaching out from Jerusalem throughout Judea, Samaria and, if not to the ends of the earth quite yet, at least into Syria.

C H A P T E R 5

Paul Versus Jesus

P aul, having been remarkably quiet for the first four
chapters of a book with his name in the title, finally
appears in the story, with a bloody vengeance.

He had little to do with the actual killing of Stephen.
All that Acts says is that he looked after the coats of the
men who stoned him, and approved of what they did. Why,
if he was there, he took no part in the stoning, we are not
told; presumably not for legal reasons, as the whole thing
was illegal under Roman law anyway.

Nevertheless he joined the general onslaught against
the church with a holy passion. He seems to have taken
a leading role in the campaign, if Acts is right that the
church throughout Palestine had peace when he stopped.
He did little in Jerusalem, though, little enough that by
the time of his conversion the churches of Judea did
not know his face. His efforts were further afield. After
all, the Sadducees were taking care of the Jerusalem
Christians, and were not interested in pursuing them
outside their constituency of Judea.

Paul was keen to stop them spreading their
blasphemies among foreign Jewish communities, but as
a Pharisee he had no power or authority to attack them
himself. Local synagogues, however, did have the power to
arrest and punish errant members, so Paul got a letter of
introduction from the temple authorities, and set off
round the synagogues of northern Palestine and Syria,
persuading the local authorities to let him help them deal
with the heretics.

How extensive and prolonged this campaign was, we
do not know. Paul mentions as briefly as possible the fact
of his past crimes against the body of Christ, and Acts can
tell us little more.

The more important question is why. What compelled him to try to annihilate Christianity? He would hardly have the same motivation as the Sadducees: as a Pharisee he would by no means object in principle to such ideas as the messiah, the kingdom of God or the resurrection, as the Jerusalem priests did.

The basic answer why, Paul gives us himself: zeal for the Lord. It was the most perfect expression of his devotion to the ways of Israel's God. His list of reasons for being confident in his standing before God in his pre-Christian days culminates thus: 'as for zeal, a persecutor of the church; as to righteousness under the Law, blameless'. Far from going outside the Law in his attacks, he was fulfilling its most rigorous demands. Similarly, the biographical passage in Galatians says, 'You have heard, no doubt, of my earlier life in Judaism. I was violently persecuting the church of God and was trying to destroy it. I advanced in Judaism beyond many among my people of the same age, for I was more zealous for the traditions of my ancestors.' So again his violence demonstrates how he outstripped his fellows in zeal.

'I was violently persecuting the church of God and was trying to destroy it.'

PAUL, GALATIANS 1:13

This word 'zeal' meant rather more for first-century Jews than it does to us today. While it could simply mean 'enthusiasm', in the Jewish scriptures it is most often used specifically in connection with the Law and the temple, and is as often as not manifest in the killing of those who undermine them. The 'Zealots' were not merely people who prayed more than fellow Jews, they were terrorists against the rule of pagan Rome. The only time the word 'zeal' is used in connection with Jesus is when he 'cleansed' the temple, overturning furniture and brandishing a whip. When Paul tells the Jerusalem mob that he was brought up as 'zealous for God as you are today', it is because they have just tried to beat him to death for allegedly teaching against the Jewish people, their Law and their temple.

So Paul reinforces what we see in Acts, suggesting that he, like many others in Jerusalem, was driven to righteous violence by Christians who seemed to believe that Jesus had somehow eclipsed the Law and the temple as the centre of the Jewish faith.

But Christianity was more than just a deviant sect to Paul. To understand more exactly what drove him,

Paul and Jesus

Did Paul distort the faith of Jesus and reinvent Christianity? His letters contain astonishingly few of Jesus' teachings – no parables, no Lord's Prayer – and virtually no information about his life, apart from his death and resurrection. Not being under the law of Moses was a major theme of Paul's that Jesus never taught, while Paul seems to neglect Jesus' central theme, the kingdom of God. Is this because he received his gospel directly from God, as he saw it, and 'did not confer with any human being'?

There is something in this, but another side to it too. There are actually more quotations from Jesus in Paul than in any other first-century writings outside the Gospels, including those in the names of James, Peter and John. Paul's letters are only one small corner of his actual teaching. The crucifixion and resurrection were for Paul the climax of history, inverting his world and not eclipsing but overshadowing everything else in the life of Jesus. Jesus' teaching was addressed to Palestinian Jews, so Paul had to adapt things considerably to translate his kingdom into the Gentile world.

It is hard to deny that Christianity took a significant change of direction under Paul, but there is no reason this could not be a legitimate development that Jesus would have welcomed.

compare it with the point of view of those who overcame their prejudices to give Jesus the benefit of the doubt. Jesus' reinterpretation of Judaism was highly controversial – but then did his miracles not confirm that he was God's messiah, with the authority to speak for him, however shocking his message? Then, when instead of casting God's enemies out of Israel and establishing the new holy kingdom, he was killed by those enemies in the most shameful way possible, it did seem that God had denied Jesus' messianic claims – and yet if God had then raised Jesus from the dead, surely the verdict must be reversed again. If there was any possibility that the story of his

A crucifixion mosaic on an interior wall of St Peter's Cathedral, Bremen.

resurrection was true, then the counsel of the leading Pharisee Gamaliel in Acts makes a lot of sense: 'Keep away from these men and leave them alone; because if this plan or this undertaking is of human origin, it will fail; but if it is of God, you will not be able to overthrow them – in that case you may even be found fighting against God!'

For Paul, by contrast, the law of Moses, as interpreted by the scribes and Pharisees, was so unassailable that Jesus' attitude to it was unquestionably blasphemous. Someone so overindulgent could not possibly be the messiah, and so no miracle he performed could prove his credentials, but rather the opposite: as the Pharisees in the Gospels say, 'He has Beelzebul, and by the ruler of the demons he casts out demons.' Jesus' death was the final proof that he was an enemy of the Lord, crushed by his righteous judgment, for the law of Moses declares, 'Anyone hung on a tree is under God's curse.' This false messiah, supposedly bringing in the day of resurrection and the kingdom of God, was, in fact, in the power of the evil one, trying to overturn the very things that the true messiah would come to champion: Jesus was, quite literally, the Antichrist. Those spreading lies about his resurrection to justify subverting the Law and temple had to be stopped.

On the Road

And so Paul, the nemesis of the Christian movement, using every means available to him to eradicate it, set off to Damascus in Syria to extend his campaign of violence and imprisonment. By the time he arrived there, he was a Christian. We are now a few years after the death of Jesus, probably AD 33.

Even at this most crucial, transforming and iconic moment of Paul's life, what happened is hard to say. Considering that it is probably the most celebrated event in Christian history outside the life of Jesus, Paul's own account breezes past it at appalling speed. Having mentioned his previous life of zeal and persecution, he says, 'But when God, who had set me apart before I was born and called me through his grace, was pleased to reveal his Son to me, so that I might proclaim him among the Gentiles, I did not confer with any human being...' This tells us nothing beyond the bare fact that he was converted. For all we know from this, it might have happened through reading a book, talking with Christians or just thinking things through.

Elsewhere, though, Paul tells us that he at some point met the risen Jesus. Reminding the Corinthian church about the various resurrection appearances to the apostles, he ends the list with his own encounter: 'last of all, as to one untimely born, he also appeared to me'. Earlier he asks them, 'Am I not an apostle? Have I not seen Jesus our Lord?' So Paul, not surprisingly, confirms the basic point of Acts' story, that he was converted by an encounter with the risen Lord.

Acts, in contrast, tells the story at some length three times over. In addition to the event itself, Paul afterwards recounts it to the Jewish mob and at his Roman trial,

Three scenes
from Paul's
conversion.
1. Paul, with a
letter from the
high priest,
rounds up
Christians;
2. Paul's vision
of Christ on
the road to
Damascus;
3. Paul is led
into Damascus
by Ananias.
Fourteenth-
century
Serbian wall
painting.

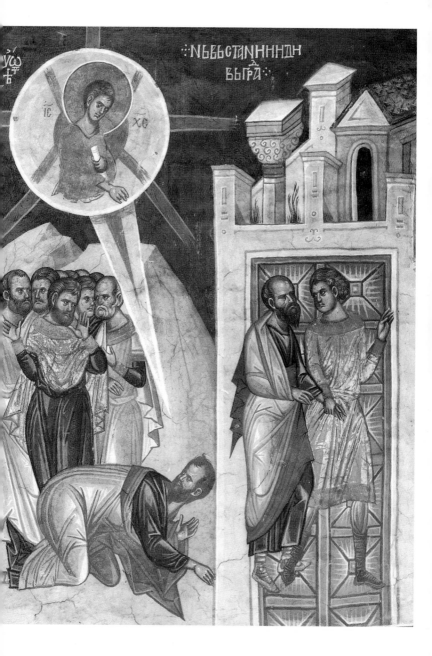

ᲘᲜ ΒЬСΤΑΝΝΝΝΔΗ
ΒЬΓΡΑ

adding many details that we do not get from Paul's letters. According to Acts, Paul was on the road to Damascus with a group of men, when a blinding light – quite literally in Paul's case – broke on them. Falling to the ground, Paul hears the voice of Jesus, saying in Aramaic, 'Saul, Saul, why do you persecute me?'

'Who are you, Lord?' asks Paul. What a question. It sounds somewhat confused, and yet it perfectly sums up the terrible implications of the encounter. Could it be that the Lord Paul thought he was serving in his campaign was in fact the one he was attacking? Had he, the great scholar of the faith, mistaken the messiah for the Antichrist? Could the Lord of glory who now appeared to him also be the one who had been cursed by God in his shameful death? And if Paul's exemplary obedience to the law of the Lord culminated in this personal epiphany – where he was accused of persecuting him – who was the Lord?

'I am Jesus whom you are persecuting,' he is told.

In the last version of the story in Acts, Jesus then appoints him as a missionary to the Gentiles; in the other shorter accounts he merely tells him to go into the city and await further instructions. Blinded by the light of the world, Paul is led by his companions into Damascus. For three days, Acts tells us, he was in darkness, eating and drinking nothing. Can we even imagine the spiritual turmoil? On the third day, God sent Ananias, one of the Damascus Christians, to him, who healed his blindness and baptized him in the name of Jesus the messiah.

What had happened? It is often said – not least by Luke – that Paul had a vision of Jesus. One wonders whether Paul would have been satisfied with that description, as he insists that he had an encounter with the resurrected Jesus of the same kind as the other apostles' meeting. The stories of these earlier appearances which were later compiled in the Gospels – and were certainly already a major feature of Christian preaching – are unanimous that it was a solid, flesh-and-blood man that they met, and in Paul's teaching resurrection is a

'We cannot call his conversion anything but a miracle; and the miracle appears all the greater when we remember that in this revulsion of his consciousness he broke through the barriers of Judaism in to the universalism of Christianity.'

F.C. BAUR,
NINETEENTH
CENTURY

bodily thing. One would assume, therefore, that Paul saw his encounter as more than a mere vision.

One might argue that this is too modern a distinction for Paul. First-century Jews did not consider visions of God or angels to be 'all in the head' in contrast to a real, verifiable appearance. Acts' conversion story is very much in the tradition of the calling of the biblical prophets – the light, the falling to the ground, the mission from God – and such stories make little or no distinction between vision and direct encounter.

Acts' triplicate account of the incident must after all reflect something of Paul's own telling of the story, unless we accept that the author had never heard an authentic account of Paul's conversion, which is hard to credit. And even Acts presents the event as something more objective than a personal vision, in that the men with Paul also saw the light, though the three accounts disagree as to whether they heard the voice too. The best interpretation is probably that the letters and Acts retell the same basic story with a different spin or interpretation, Paul on this occasion presenting it as a resurrection appearance, Acts more as a prophetic calling.

Paul in Christian art

Unfortunately for artists, there is no physical description of anyone in the New Testament. For Paul, the late second-century *Acts of Paul* tries to make up for this oversight. It describes him as short, balding and bandy-legged, with meeting eyebrows and a hooked nose. It hardly sounds flattering, which might suggest it is accurate, although some argue that such features were considered majestic in the ancient world.

Consequently Paul is usually depicted with receding hairline in art, but with a dark, bushy beard to compensate. He is traditionally seen with a sword and a book, reflecting his manner of execution and his contribution to scripture. Pictures of his conversion generally show him falling from a horse, though no horse is mentioned in Acts.

Liberation from the Law?

Was Paul's conversion as sudden and unprepared for as
one might assume from Acts? Luke might seem to suggest
that Paul's conversion was utterly out of the blue, with
no background at all to prepare the way for it. Was there
more to it than that?

Here we are walking through the back door of the
hottest debate in contemporary Pauline studies. The
traditional understanding, at least among Protestants, is
that Paul's conversion came as the climax to a long and
depressingly futile struggle to save his soul by keeping the
law of Moses perfectly. In this view, that is what Judaism

Ananias baptizes
Paul, apparently
in a babies' font.
A twelfth-century
Byzantine mosaic.

was all about, 'salvation by works': the only stairway to heaven it offered was faultless obedience to the Law, the one catch being that this is impossible.

The main shaper of this understanding is Martin Luther, who himself had a long, desperate struggle to appease God by the irreproachable holiness of his life according to the demands of the Roman Catholic spirituality in which he had been trained. He was liberated from this by the writings of Paul, where he read, as he understood it, that we are saved not by our irreproachable life or holy deeds but merely by having faith in Christ. It became natural for those who followed him to assume that Paul's pre-Christian life had been, like Luther's, an unavailing labour to keep the impossible demands of the Law, until he discovered that he could be made righteous in God's sight merely by accepting what Jesus had achieved on his behalf.

This interpretation of Paul's conversion was shaken by the North American scholar E.P. Sanders in the 1970s. Sanders argued that this was a hopelessly negative and stereotyped view of first-century Judaism, which in fact did not teach 'justification by works' at all. Instead it was all about covenant. God, out of sheer goodness, chose the Jewish people to be his and brought them into a loving relationship with him; living by the Law was a way for the Jews to respond to God's graciousness, and to remain in his good books, not what they had to do to gain his acceptance in the first place.

We will look at this in more depth when we explore Paul's later teaching on justification, but as far as it concerns his conversion, Sanders's reinterpretation seems irresistible. The passages in which Paul definitely talks about his pre-Christian past never suggest that it was a futile, unhappy struggle to reach an impossible standard. Quite the opposite. He boasts of his success: 'as to righteousness under the Law, blameless'. Conversion for Paul was not like trading in an old car with which he had been having increasing problems, as soon as he came across a better model; he was cruising to Damascus in the car of his dreams, when he had a head-on collision. As Sanders puts it, 'this is what Paul finds wrong with Judaism: it is not Christianity'.

This being the case, it is even debated whether Paul underwent a conversion at all. This is on the whole a question of words, I think: if by 'conversion' we mean that he utterly abandoned the Jewish faith and turned to a completely different one, certainly he did not; if it means that he went through a radical change of thinking and direction, and joined a new religious community, certainly he did.

So, Paul's conversion was sudden and unprepared for, in the sense that it was not the culmination of a disillusionment with Judaism. We might still wonder, though, whether anything else helped to prepare the way. Personal contacts are almost always crucial to religious conversion, and Paul had certainly met Christians during his attacks on them at least. In the coming generations, the strength and courage with which Christians went to their death rather than deny Jesus repeatedly made a great impression on their enemies, and one can well imagine that Paul's confidence in the evil of Christianity was challenged by the heroic sufferings of his victims, and possibly, as he preached against them, by their self-defence.

But whatever part this may have played in Paul's change of heart, for the one central factor we can do nothing better at this distance than accept Paul's story, however we may explain or interpret it: Jesus appeared to him.

The Convert

So Paul is in Damascus and Jesus is the messiah. It is no exaggeration to say that for Paul the world, and more besides, has turned upside down, and he has a great deal of thinking to do – about the messiah, the coming reign of the Lord, the hope of Israel, the Law, the temple, and above all the great question that he never expected to ask, 'Who are you, Lord?'

Paul's activity at this point is no clearer than ever. He offers more information about his movements now, in Galatians, than at any other stage of his life, and on oath before God too, as if to forestall any question of its reliability. But it is bare and sketchy and mostly concerned with the question of when he met other apostles, not the most pressing issue for us. Acts tells the story too, but Paul rather undermines its version at one point, only to offer striking confirmation at another.

In Damascus

Paul says that after an early visit to Arabia – for prayer and reflection, one supposes – he stayed for three years in Damascus. (In Semitic idiom this could mean almost anything between one and three years, any part of a year counting as one year.) Acts adds that his preaching grew increasingly powerful as he argued with his fellow Jews that Jesus was the messiah. And that is all the information we have about a period quite possibly as long as the whole previous story of the church from the death of Jesus.

Whether the Christians were initially suspicious of Paul's alleged conversion, we are not told. They may well have been, but if so it cannot have lasted long: even if he had wanted to infiltrate the community, such a man could no more have declared 'Jesus is Lord' with his fingers crossed and been baptized in his name, than a Christian could have denied Jesus and sacrificed to Caesar.

Paul will have prayed and worshipped with the believers he came to crush, and attended synagogues with them and other Jews. He will have listened to the Christians' stories of Jesus with a new sympathy, and read the scriptures in a new light trying to make sense of the crucified messiah. We know that he proclaimed his conversion and preached the resurrection of Jesus.

For the Damascus Christians it must have been an unbelievable joy. A great, dangerous enemy of the church

A seventeenth-
century view of
Damascus.

was not just disposed of, but won over to their own mission. It was, apart from anything, the greatest trophy conversion in history.

It was as galling to Paul's former friends, of course, as it was delightful for the Christians, and a blasphemous betrayal. Consequently, Paul's stay in Damascus ended with him running for his life. The controversy he was stirring up came to the attention of the governor of Damascus, who, allegedly on the request of influential Jewish opponents of Christianity, sent soldiers to arrest him. They were stationed on the city gates to seize him, but the plan was leaked to the Christians, so they smuggled Paul out by hiding him in a basket and lowering it out of a window in the city wall.

This basket story, which is told in Acts, is also recounted by Paul, making for a useful illustration of the value of Acts. On the one hand the fact that such a random, casual reminiscence from Paul confirms Acts' account in substance and in several details affirms Luke's general reliability. On the other hand, the fact that Paul ascribes the attempted arrest to the governor of Damascus and Acts ascribes it to the Jews, suggests that Luke is willing to simplify the story, or perhaps even to fill in the gaps in his information with guesswork. It also supports the criticism that he is too ready to portray non-Christian Jews as villains, which may make us more cautious about his accounts of Jewish persecutions elsewhere.

Paul escapes from Damascus in a basket. A painting from San Proculo, Naturno, Italy.

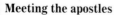

Meeting the apostles

On escape from Damascus, Paul went to Jerusalem. This much Galatians and Acts

Peter with the key to the kingdom of heaven and Paul with the sword of martyrdom. A fifteenth-century Italian fresco.

agree on, but their accounts of the visit are rather different. Acts tells us that when Paul turned up and tried to join the Christians they refused to believe him, until one of them introduced him to the apostles. He then 'went in and out among them' preaching fearlessly about Jesus, until he had to move on again to avoid assassination. In Galatians, on the other hand, Paul swears that he stayed just fifteen days with Peter, and 'did not see another apostle except James, the Lord's brother'.

It is possible to harmonize these tensions between Paul and Luke. Acts may give the impression of a longer visit than a fortnight, but this is not stated, and 'the apostles' could refer to a welcoming committee of just Peter and James. What is most questionable about Acts' account is the idea that the Jerusalem church was still suspicious that Paul was trying to infiltrate them. Though Paul says nothing to imply that he was welcomed with open arms, it does seem intrinsically improbable that the Jerusalem church should still distrust his conversion after three years of Christian preaching from him. To be sure he had been in a different country, but Damascus is only 150 miles from Jerusalem, communications were good, and the news that 'The one who formerly was persecuting us is now proclaiming the faith he once tried to destroy' could not possibly have been slow in coming. The most likely explanation is that Luke was not aware that Paul had stayed as long as three years in Damascus, and so, knowing that Paul was brought to the apostles by one of the believers, assumed this was necessary because they were still afraid of him. Perhaps he combined this event with stories of other Christians such as those in Damascus being afraid of Paul earlier.

Barnabas

Barnabas was the most important friend of Paul's Christian life, though they were only friends for the first half of it. He was a dispersion Jew born in Cyprus, of the tribe of Levi; his background was probably a mixture of devout Judaism and Greek culture similar to Paul's own. He was a landowner, presumably in Jerusalem, as he first appears in Acts early on, selling a field to contribute to church funds. Other members of his family were also Jerusalem Christians: his aunt Mary had a house there where many met to pray, and her son John Mark would later accompany Paul and Barnabas on their travels, before – according to tradition – compiling Peter's stories of Jesus into the first Gospel.

It was Barnabas who asked Paul to help lead the church at Antioch, joined him on their first missionary journey and testified with him at the Jerusalem council. Shortly afterwards they fell out over personal and theological matters and went their separate ways, at which point Barnabas fades out of history. A letter from around AD 100 was (probably falsely) attributed to him.

The Christian who introduced Paul to Peter was a man named Joseph, better known by his nickname Barnabas, 'son of encouragement'. Being a Greek-speaking Christian, he may well have been among those who fled to Damascus to escape the attacks in Jerusalem, and so having seen Paul's Christian faith in action was able to vouch for him to Peter and James. Or maybe he was simply being a son of encouragement. Either way, thanks to Barnabas, Paul finally met Peter and stayed for two weeks in his lodgings.

What a meeting! The leader of the church gives shelter and protection to the man who was last seen trying to destroy it. The great theologian and architect of the faith talks with Jesus' right-hand man. The fervent new missionary of the risen Lord compares notes with the man who ate and slept and travelled with Jesus for three years. The Galilean fisherman breaks bread with the Asia Minor tentmaker.

Sadly, we know nothing at all of their conversation. All we know is that once again Paul preached openly and that again his former friends tried to kill him. This is a measure of how powerful his message was, but also how abrasive and inflammatory he was. Quite certain of his controversial beliefs, he would leave a trail of aggravation and destruction around the Mediterranean. Again the Christians got Paul out of the city, and this time sent him north back home to Tarsus.

It would be almost fourteen years before Paul saw Jerusalem again, and by then Christianity would have taken arguably the most radical change of direction in its 2,000-year history.

Antioch

The Christian church in Antioch was established during the great assault by Paul and his associates. Nicolaus, one of the seven Hellenistic leaders in Jerusalem, is named in Acts as an Antiochene, a Gentile by birth who had already converted to Judaism before becoming a Christian. It may possibly have been he who, finding Jerusalem too dangerous, went home to Antioch and started telling people there about the resurrection of the messiah.

It was in this church that something happened with incalculable results for the stories of Paul's life, of Christianity and of the world. With hindsight, it may seem natural, inevitable even, that the gospel of Jesus should embrace Gentiles as well as Jews, but to Christians at the time it was not so obvious. Why should the news that the Jews' messiah had come and been rejected, executed and resurrected suddenly make non-Jews more

Antioch

Antioch, the capital of Syria, was one of the largest cities in the Roman empire, a thriving cosmopolitan place 300 miles north of Jerusalem, where between seven and twenty per cent of the population were Jews. It was a natural second home for Christianity, the place where it first started to change from a Jewish sect into a world religion and appropriately, therefore, the place where the name 'Christian' was born. It was to be one of the most important cities in the first millennium of Christian history, with many of the heated debates that forged Christian theology being hammered out between the schools of Antioch and Alexandria.

eager than before to accept the Jewish religion? But, in multi-cultural Antioch, the Christians did indeed start spreading the message among Gentiles as well as their fellow Jews. And it was a success. Just ten years after the death of Jesus the first mixed-race church was created, and the movement had leapt from the Galilean countryside into the Roman world. Christianity was no longer just another new Jewish movement.

A huge question now faced the Antioch church: where did these non-Jewish Christians stand in relation to the law of Moses? There was no question about the fact that in converting to Christianity they were embracing the Jewish faith: all Christians had always seen their religion as the perfection of Judaism, not its new rival. Should Gentiles who joined therefore be expected to keep the Law in all its fullness?

'Blessed are you for not having made me a Gentile.'

JEWISH MORNING
PRAYER

One would assume so. But then those who had become believers in the Jewish God previously and joined the synagogue community had not necessarily had to. Some certainly were circumcised into the fullness of the Law, becoming in effect Jews, but others were content merely to be God-fearers.

In all probability, the Antioch church accepted Gentile converts on either basis, and so some may well have been circumcised. But if uncircumcised Gentiles also were being baptized into the church – into the body of Christ as Paul would put it – forgiven their sins, eligible to share communion and guaranteed salvation when the Lord returned, then they might be forgiven for thinking that they had all they needed, that circumcision and the law of Moses were burdens not worth their weight. And the more Gentiles became Christians without observing the Law, the more redundant it must have seemed to those who came after. We have seen the Greek-speaking Jews of the dispersion apparently developing a controversially dismissive attitude to the Law even in the all-Jewish environment of Jerusalem; it is not surprising to see them take this further when it came to mission to the Gentiles in Roman Antioch.

However, it was not only a question of leniency to Gentile Christians. The Jewish believers were compromising their own obedience to the law of Moses, because it forbade eating with the ritually unclean – and if they shared bread and wine with the uncircumcised then that is precisely what they were doing.

News that the Lord was now drawing in the Gentiles reached Jerusalem soon enough. How the Aramaic Christians there reacted is hard to say. It should have been occasion for rejoicing: it was one of the great hopes of the Jews that one day all the nations would join them in worshipping the one true God. The prophets had promised it:

Many nations shall come, and say:
'Come, let us go up to the mountain of the Lord,
to the house of the God of Jacob;
that he may teach us his ways
and we may walk in his paths.'
For out of Zion shall go forth the Law,
and the word of the Lord from Jerusalem.
MICAH 4:2

But, of course, this vision involved the Gentiles submitting to the law of Moses, the *sine qua non* of knowing and following the Lord. It was at the very centre of the Jewish faith, and so Jews no more expected the nations to come to God without the Law than modern Christian missionaries would expect people to become Christians without accepting the Bible. If the Jerusalem Christians realized that the Antiochenes were trying to bypass the Law, many must have had grave reservations. When the full facts emerged, many – notably James the Righteous, Jesus' brother, it seems – were seriously unhappy.

Others such as Peter were more sympathetic, however. Acts brings together many stories about him at this point, although they give the impression of perhaps being somewhat legendary. There is probably, however, bearing in mind his later activity, a factual basis to the story of his causing a stir by eating with the centurion Cornelius. Being a Gentile God-fearer, Cornelius was eligible to worship with Jews but not to eat with them, and Acts links the incident with a vision in which Jesus tells Peter to eat unclean food.

Peter had after all been as close to Jesus as any other person, and – according to Mark's Gospel, which is supposedly comprised of his reminiscences – Jesus set very little store by ritual cleanliness, considering it more important to welcome the unclean (such as tax collectors,

St Philip Baptizing the Eunuch, by Claude Lorrain, 1677.

prostitutes, haemorrhaging women and lepers) into the kingdom of God than to steer clear of them. Jesus insisted that words and deeds are more important than food, and thereby, according to the interpretation recorded in Mark, declared all food clean.

It is no surprise to hear such stories told about Greek-speaking Christians too, such as Philip's baptism of an Ethiopian who was not only Gentile but doubly unclean by virtue of being a eunuch.

Reactions to the news from Antioch would be expected to vary, then, in proportion to whether one accepted the radically inclusive understanding of the Law taught by Jesus according to the synoptic tradition.

The most enthusiastic response was from Barnabas, who left Jerusalem and joined the Antioch church. He became its main leader, along with three men: Simeon Niger ('the dark'), maybe an African Jew; Lucius, a Greek-speaking African from Cyrene on what is now the coast of Libya; and a Jewish aristocrat, Menachem (or Manaen in Greek), who had been a courtier of King Herod.

While working in Antioch, Barnabas decided that the church needed another pair of hands, and that the best available were Paul's. What Paul had done to warrant this we do not know. It is anywhere between two and fourteen years, depending on how you do the arithmetic, since we last saw him leaving Jerusalem for Cilicia, though probably at the lower end of the scale, so that we are now around AD 40. We really have no idea what has been happening to him. This period of his life, however long, is a blank.

According to later legend he devoted the time to monastic-style study and contemplation to prepare for his coming mission. This seems unlikely considering that in all we see of him before and after he is passionately active and preaching at every opportunity. One would assume that he has been engaging in evangelism one way or another, but to Jews or Gentiles, and successfully or unsuccessfully? The fact that he was chosen by Barnabas for the work in Antioch would suggest that he had been preaching successfully to Gentiles, while the fact that no record survives of any such success, in the form of letters or churches, would suggest otherwise. The fact that in Galatians Paul sees himself as called to the Gentiles at his very conversion suggests that he preached to them from the start, but as he is writing this many years later we cannot tell how much the recollection is influenced by the shape of his career after being brought to Antioch.

Doubtless Paul's powers as a theologian were also valuable to the Antioch church, and he became the fifth member of their team of prophets and teachers. What their roles were as 'prophets and teachers' is not entirely clear. There were many different job titles at different times and places in the early church with varying meanings – apostle, elder, pastor, evangelist, deacon (or 'servant'), bishop (or 'overseer'), as well as prophet and teacher – and it is probably unwise to read too much into them. 'Prophet' suggests something more charismatic, bringing messages from God to address the present situation maybe, while 'teacher' might be more concerned with matters of doctrine; but then Paul insists most emphatically that his doctrine is also an urgent message from God, so the distinction is not rigid. Probably both teaching and prophesying overlapped with what we would today call preaching. What precisely Paul preached in Antioch is the subject of the next chapter.

Paul Preaches

We are given a fairly good indication of what Paul taught at Antioch in 1 and 2 Thessalonians, probably his earliest letters. Though they were written years later, they were intended to remind churches similar to the one in Antioch of what he had first taught them, and so offer a useful insight into the basics of Paul's preaching.

Paul did not ask Gentile converts to follow the law of Moses, as we know, so which elements of the Jewish faith should they adopt? First of all, they must worship one God. It was natural for pagans to assume that they could worship the Jewish Lord as supreme God and continue to offer sacrifices to their other gods – whether to appease them or other pagans. But Paul was adamant: this was completely unacceptable. 'Flee from the worship of idols', he told them. When he was in Thessalonica, he was delighted that his converts 'turned to God from idols, to serve a living and true God'. One of the most insistent themes of the Hebrew scriptures was that the worship of false gods is incompatible with the worship of the one true God. Whether the pagans were really worshipping evil spirits or empty space, first-century Judaism seems undecided – either alternative served well depending on whom you were arguing against. Paul seems to lean to the former: 'What pagans sacrifice, they sacrifice to demons,' he would later warn the Corinthians, though also conceding 'No idol in the world really exists.' Either way the rule is clear: 'For us there is one God.'

The other way in which he taught Gentile converts to embrace Judaism was in the sphere of personal morality. The greatest difference between pagans and Jews here was in the matter of sex. Judaism had rather stricter

'His preaching was a blazing fire carrying all before it. It was the sun rising in full glory. Unbelief was consumed by it, wrong beliefs fled away, and the truth was made manifest, like a great candle lighting the whole world with its bright flame.'

BERNARDINE OF SIENA, FIFTEENTH CENTURY

Paul and English

A number of Paul's phrases have proved catchy enough to pass, via the Authorized Version, into our everyday language. Some are so common that we have no idea we are quoting Paul, and some have come to mean something quite different from what Paul meant. For example:

A law unto themselves (Romans 2:14)

Hope against hope (Romans 4:18)

The powers that be (Romans 13:1)

A thorn in the flesh (2 Corinthians 12:7)

Fall from grace (Galatians 5:4)

You reap what you sow (Galatians 6:7)

The love of money is the root of all evil (1 Timothy 6:10)

Fight the good fight (1 Timothy 6:12)

standards, confining sex absolutely to marriage, whereas the Hellenistic society of the empire generally accepted prostitution and homosexuality quite happily, and only condemned adultery when it involved a married woman (i.e. when it was a violation of a husband's rights).

Paul insisted that Gentile converts accept Jewish standards. 'You know what instructions we gave you through the Lord Jesus...' he reminds the Thessalonians, 'that you abstain from fornication; that each one of you know how to control your own body with holiness and honour, not with lustful passion, like the Gentiles who do not know God'. Of course he also exhorted them to live impeccable lives in every other way – and especially to love one another as brothers and sisters – but this was the area where they most had to change their values.

Who Jesus was

More than anything, Paul preached to Christians and non-Christians, Jewish and Gentile, about Jesus. He proclaimed

A priest sacrifices to the goddess Cybele, c. second century AD, sandstone relief.

Jesus as Christ, Lord and Son of God. He uses these terms constantly in his letters, but never says much to explain them, so we do not know how much he 'unpacked' them for his audience and how much they were just accepted as impressive titles.

'Christ' is simply the Greek translation of 'messiah' (both meaning 'the anointed') but in the Greek-speaking churches it had very quickly become more or less a part of Jesus' name, as it is for us today. Paul, like other Greek-speaking Christians, talks constantly of 'Jesus Christ', 'Christ Jesus', etc., but never in his letters talks about Jesus being 'the Christ'. Doubtless the influx of Gentile Christians who were happy enough to use the title with little idea of what it had meant to Jews encouraged this process. And one imagines that Jesus' actual achievement was so different from what had been expected of the messiah that Paul saw little need to educate his converts in expectations that he himself had had to unlearn: little would be served by giving Gentiles of the Roman empire the impression that Jesus was a failed Palestinian freedom fighter. If they understood 'Jesus Christ' as simply 'King Jesus', they would not be too far from Paul's meaning.

'Son of God' is another term open to different interpretations. We must be clear straight away that 'Son of God' is not the same as 'God the Son', the second person of the Trinity. No first-century Christian thought in those terms, however appropriate they may be as a later development in Christian understanding.

'Son of' was a common figure of speech in Hebrew and Aramaic, describing a man's character rather than his birth or personal relationships. We have already met Barnabas, the 'son of encouragement'. Similarly Jesus nicknamed James and John 'the sons of thunder'. Both Judas Iscariot and the coming 'lawless one' predicted by Paul are called 'the son of destruction', and in Acts the magician Bar-Jesus is called a 'son of the devil'. So to call someone 'the Son of God' in this context may suggest a man extraordinarily close to God, in tune with his ways and full of his spirit, wisdom and power, but the phrase on its own would not necessarily mean he was 'eternally begotten of the Father', as the Nicene creed puts it, 'God from God, Light from Light'.

In fact, the Jewish scriptures call angels, the king of Israel and Israel as a whole sons of God. In first-century Israel, it seems the term was extended to the coming messiah and to various other especially righteous men, such as the patriarch Joseph. Paul himself calls both Christians and the Jewish people sons of God, and Jesus says that peacemakers are sons of God.

That said, it is clear that Paul presented Jesus as being God's Son in a unique way, by no means just another great man of God. However, since especially in his early work he uses the term 'Son' little and explains it less (it occurs only once in the Thessalonian letters), we should not be too quick to assume that Paul explained it to Antioch in the same language later Christians might use.

As for how the Gentile Christians understood it, Roman emperors and other great men were called sons of God, reflecting their divine appointment and power. So again, if Christians applied the same idea to Jesus, as the true God's true emperor, and reflecting his power and glory, they would have understood something at least of what Paul was saying.

'Lord' was Paul's favourite title for Jesus. In 1 Thessalonians he calls him 'Christ' nine times, 'Son' once, and 'Lord' twenty-four times. We know that the term was used before Paul's time by the church in Palestine, because, in what is probably the earliest scrap of Christian liturgy in existence, Paul quotes in 1 Corinthians from the Aramaic service the invocation 'Maranatha!' ('Come, Lord!')

The head of Emperor Augustus, from Pergamum.

'Lord' was a powerful and loaded term with resonances for both Jews and Gentiles. It was what N.T. Wright calls 'fighting talk'. For Gentiles, on the one hand, it may have seemed a rather risky term, presenting Jesus as a rival to the lord of the earth, Caesar – and this is precisely what Paul insisted he was. Allegiance to Jesus overrode every other commitment and demanded one's whole life.

For Jews, on the other hand, 'Lord' was the name of
their God. 'Hear, O Israel', their prayers exhorted them
morning and evening, 'The Lord is our God, the Lord
alone.' Their ultimate devotion to this divine Lord above
all pretenders – including Lord Caesar – was one for which
many Jews were willing to shed blood, whether others' or
their own. So for Christians constantly to proclaim Jesus
as the Lord was a challenge, to say the least. But rather
than shade the controversial implications of this, Paul
spotlit them. From the start, his writings are full of
phrases such as 'God the Father and the Lord Jesus
Christ' – including the very first verse of 1 Thessalonians.
For Paul the Jew, God was Father and Lord; for Paul the
Christian Jew, God's Lordship was now in some sense
shared with Jesus.

What Jesus did

At least as important for Paul as who Jesus was, however,
was what he had done, and was going to do. The words of
the Mass sum up Paul's teaching perfectly: 'Christ has
died. Christ is risen. Christ shall come again.'

Once more we can see Paul's teaching already
enshrined in earlier liturgy that he quotes. He is almost
certainly reciting a creed (either one from the Greek-
speaking church, or an Aramaic one that he translates
himself) when he reminds the Corinthians of the teaching
he passed on to them from those who passed it on to him:

*that Christ died for our sins in accordance with the
scriptures, and that he was buried, and that he was raised
on the third day in accordance with the scriptures, and that
he appeared to Cephas, and then the twelve.*

1 CORINTHIANS 15:3–5

Concerning the death of Christ, Paul reminds the
Thessalonians that they will be saved 'through the Lord
Jesus Christ who died for us'. What precisely Jesus' death
achieved for us and how – the meaning and purpose of the

crucifixion – is, of course, one of the great questions of Christianity, but in the Thessalonian letters, he says no more than this.

Paul saw the resurrection in a very Jewish way – not simply as a miracle that set God's sign of approval on the life of Jesus, but as an advance on the general resurrection of God's people. As we have seen, many Jews were eagerly awaiting the coming rule of God, when Israel would be liberated and restored to its former glory and holiness, and those who were dead would be raised to share in the utopia. If the messiah had now come and been raised from the dead himself, then the resurrection had started. Jesus' resurrection was by no means an isolated event, but almost like the first spring flower after a long Narnian winter – 'the first fruits of those who have died' as Paul would put it in 1 Corinthians.

As a result, Jesus' resurrection is inextricably tied to his coming again in Paul's early thought. He explores this at length in both 1 and 2 Thessalonians. Since the resurrection has started, it will be completed when the rest of God's departed are also raised. Jesus will come back from heaven to accomplish this.

By the second century, it became known as Christ's 'second coming', having become so separate in time from his resurrection and elevation to heaven. But for Paul it was simply 'the coming', inseparable from what had already happened.

Understandably, therefore, Paul expected it imminently – in a matter of years maybe, but not millennia. This fact is resisted by those writers who hold that the New Testament cannot reflect any false hopes of its writers (a claim not made by those writers themselves), but it is nevertheless clearly true. More than once in 1 Thessalonians he includes himself among those 'who are alive, who are left at the coming of the Lord'.

At the same time, though, he reminds them that no one knows 'the times or the seasons'. 'The day of the Lord will come like a thief in the night,' he says, so living a sober life of faith and love in perpetual readiness is what matters.

That phrase 'the day of the Lord' reflects what Paul hoped for from Christ's coming. It was a common term among the biblical prophets, looking to a time when God would come and vindicate his people, bringing liberation and victory and righting wrongs, though Israel itself would not be exempt from his judgment. For Paul, it was now Jesus who would come as Lord. (In his later letters 'the day of the Lord' is interchangeable with 'the day of the Lord Jesus Christ' and 'the day of Christ' – another example of how Jesus had, in Christian eyes, taken the Lordship of God upon himself.) He would judge the nations and right injustice. He would also vindicate his people, proving the Christian community right in the eyes both of the unbelieving Jews and the wider world.

Missionary Travels

I t was from Antioch, after he had been there about a year, that Paul first set out on his missionary travels. This was not his own initiative: he was accompanying Barnabas, whom the Antioch church probably still considered the senior partner; and the pair were sent by the church, Acts tells us, on the inspiration of the Holy Spirit.

Such words from the Lord were evidently an important and normal part of first-century church life. Acts also mentions, for example, the prophet Agabus coming to Antioch with a prediction of famine, and Paul talks about going to Jerusalem in response to a revelation. He tells the Thessalonians to respect prophets, though not to accept what they say uncritically.

And so, while they were fasting – a regular part of Jewish religion, usually combined with prayer – and worshipping, the Antioch church was told to commission Barnabas and Paul for foreign mission, and they set off. Now Paul was an apostle not only of Christ but also of the church at Antioch. We are now at some point in the early 40s, a little over a decade after the death of Jesus.

'In every town and village, like a well-filled threshing floor, churches shot up, bursting with eager members.'

EUSEBIUS OF
CAESAREA, FOURTH
CENTURY

Cyprus

The round trip as Acts describes it was a modest one compared to Paul's later travels. They went first to Barnabas's homeland, Cyprus, and then up to Asia Minor, going round several cities in the south of the Roman province of Galatia, before returning to Antioch.

The two of them preached their way across Cyprus, from the old capital Salamis on the east coast, to the new

capital Paphos on the south-west, accompanied
by Barnabas's cousin John Mark. Cyprus was not virgin
territory for the gospel, as Greek-speaking Christians
had gone there as early as Paul's attack on the church.
Acts has no stories to tell about this leg of the journey
apart from an incident in Paphos – maybe because
Barnabas was taking the lead in his own territory, and
Acts from here on is purely the story of Paul, omitting
almost everything else.

The remains of a
bathhouse in the
gymnasium
complex at
Salamis.

In Paphos, Luke tells us that the Roman governor of
the island, Sergius Paulus, was interested enough by what
he heard of Barnabas and Paul to summon them to come
and tell him about their teachings. But when they did so,
a member of his court, a Jewish magician and purported
prophet called Bar-Jesus, spoke out against them, so Paul
called on God to blind him temporarily, which he did. The
governor was so impressed, we are told, that he became a
Christian.

They sailed from Cyprus to Asia Minor, where they
toured a number of cities in the vast province of Galatia.
Writing later to the churches that they founded, Paul
says:

*You know that it was because of a physical infirmity that I
first announced the gospel to you; though my condition put
you to the test, you did not scorn or despise me.*

GALATIANS 4:13–14

This is intriguing, and we can only guess how any kind
of ailment might have made Paul preach in Galatia. Acts
certainly knows nothing about it. The fact that Paul goes
on to say 'I know that if it were possible you would have
pulled out your eyes and given them to me' sounds like a
clue, but we are still in the dark.

The first stop that Acts mentions is the inland city of
Perga, though they may well have stopped in the seaport
of Attalia first. Luke tells us nothing of their time in Perga
either, except that for some reason John Mark left them
and returned to Jerusalem. This was apparently a very
sore point with Paul, who in later years refused to work
with him again, to the point of permanently falling out
with Barnabas who wanted to give him another chance.
Later still, Paul was reconciled to John Mark, mentioning
him as a co-worker in his letters and instructing his
followers to welcome him.

Pisidian Antioch

Heading into the province of Galatia, they visited another
city confusingly called Antioch, 100 miles north of Perga.
(At that time, there were many cities so named, after the
ruling house of Antiochus. This one is usually known as
Pisidian Antioch, despite not actually being the Antioch
that was in the region of Pisidia.)

Here Luke records a sermon of Paul's for the first
time. On the one hand, this may be because Paul was
taking more of a lead now that they were on his home
ground, a possibility backed by the fact that Acts suddenly
starts calling the pair 'Paul and Barnabas' instead of
'Barnabas and Saul'. On the other hand, both facts might
also be explained by the possibility that Luke is now
getting his information from a different source, the

previous one having focused on Barnabas, the new one, more usefully for Luke's purpose, focusing on Paul.

According to Acts, Paul preached in the Jewish synagogue before an audience of Jewish and Gentile God-fearers, who were interested enough to invite him back the following week. This second time he drew huge crowds, which Luke reckons made his original Jewish audience jealous, and they violently denounced his teachings. Paul and Barnabas therefore turned their backs on the Jews of Pisidian Antioch and preached to the Gentiles, many of whom were converted, until Jewish attacks forced them to move on.

This is the typical pattern of Paul's preaching in Acts: the gospel is offered first to the Jews, and only when they reject it does he go to the Gentiles. Many scholars have doubted the truth of this, though. When Paul later wrote to the Galatians – to those churches he was now founding – he presented himself simply as an apostle to the Gentiles, talking of a clear division of labour between himself and Peter, the apostle to the Jews. Moreover all his letters to churches (except Romans) seem to be addressed to entirely Gentile communities, confirming,

The remains of an
aqueduct at
Pisidian Antioch.

it is said, that Paul preached only to Gentiles.

However, what these arguments demonstrate is that Paul's *converts* were largely Gentiles, and that he therefore in retrospect saw himself as the apostle to the Gentiles – not that he had never made any attempt to preach to Jews too. In fact, one of the recurrent motifs of Paul's letter to the Romans is that the gospel is first for the Jews and then for the Gentiles. Paul agonizes about his fellow Jews' rejection of Jesus, arguing that this is God's strategy to bring in the Gentiles first, ultimately provoking the Jews to come after. This does not sound like the deliberation of a man who declines to preach to fellow Jews, but of one who has failed with Jews and succeeded with Gentiles.

Iconium

From Pisidian Antioch, Paul and Barnabas made another 100-mile journey eastwards to Iconium (modern-day Konya and a medieval capital of Turkey). Here again after initial success among both Jews and Gentiles they faced serious aggravation from the former. Because of this opposition, Luke says, the pair stayed a long time with the new

believers, continuing not only to preach the gospel but also to perform miracles to show their credentials.

Paul and Barnabas stayed in Iconium until they had made themselves unwelcome enough for Jewish and Gentile opponents to unite in arranging a stoning for them.

Lystra and Derbe: mistaken for gods

When they heard about this, they escaped south and toured the region of Lyconia. In the town of Lystra, Paul and Barnabas had the novel experience of being mistaken for pagan gods. According to a story preserved in Ovid, an old couple in this region gave hospitality to a pair of strangers who turned out to be Zeus and Hermes, and they were richly rewarded. Acts tells us that when Paul healed a man there who had been lame from birth, the Lystrans believed that Zeus and Hermes had come again. Remembering the lesson of the legend, they sent for the

Zeus and Hermes are entertained unawares. *Jupiter and Mercury with Philemon and Baucis*, by Peter Paul Rubens, c. 1620.

Paul's miracles

Acts features several accounts of Paul performing miracles – healings, predictions, exorcisms, even raising the dead. These are often taken as evidence of the unreliability of Acts, being either legends that have grown up over the years or a creation of Luke's excitable imagination. In fact, the opposite is true. Acts' miracle stories only echo what Paul says in his letters. He reminds the Thessalonians: 'Our message of the gospel came to you not in word only, but also in power and in the Holy Spirit and with full conviction.' Similarly he reminds the Corinthians of his 'signs, wonders and mighty works'.

These are not Paul's memoirs, which we might suspect of tall stories. They are reminders to the original witnesses of what they saw for themselves. However we might explain the fact, it is impossible to deny that in his missionary travels Paul did things that were understood by onlookers as miracles, and that this was a significant factor in the success of his preaching.

priest of Zeus to bring garlands to adorn them and bulls for sacrifice.

It is interesting that it is Barnabas who is Zeus, the king of the gods, and Paul who is Hermes, the messenger. Acts attributes this to the fact that Paul was the talker. It seems at least as possible – though the two possibilities are not necessarily exclusive – that Barnabas seemed to be in charge.

As soon as Paul and Barnabas realized what was going on they were horrified, of course, tearing their clothes in the traditional Jewish symbol of protest against blasphemy, and they took the opportunity to preach against the folly of paganism.

It seems, however, that Paul and Barnabas were being followed. Their opponents from Pisidian Antioch and Iconium turned up in Lystra, intent on completing the stoning they had planned. This time they succeeded. They stoned Paul and left him for dead. (Paul confirms that he

once survived a stoning in his list of sufferings for the
gospel in 2 Corinthians, which Luke almost certainly had
not read.) His execution did him such surprisingly little
harm that, after a defiant appearance in the city, the
missionaries left on the sixty-mile journey to Derbe the
following day.

Derbe was the furthest extent of this first missionary
journey. After preaching there, Paul and Barnabas retraced
their path back to the coast via Lystra, Iconium, Pisidian
Antioch and Perga, revisiting the churches they had
founded and which had continued to face opposition. They
reinforced their teaching, appointed leaders from among
the converts to take permanent care of the churches, and
encouraged them all to keep going despite their troubles.
From Attalia they sailed home to Antioch to report on
their successes and on the spread of the gospel of Jesus
among the Gentiles.

This is the only missionary journey of Paul's recorded by
Acts before the momentous Jerusalem council and his split
with Barnabas. There may well have been others, though.

Paul's travels
with Barnabas.

For one thing, Acts is self-evidently not an exhaustive account of Paul's adventures, passing very briskly over some long periods of time – such as the one he now spent in Antioch, perhaps four or five years. What is more, Paul's list of hardships in 2 Corinthians contains many incidents not included in Acts. 'Five times I have received from the Jews the forty lashes minus one,' Paul recalls. 'Three times I was beaten with rods... Three times I was shipwrecked.' Acts has only one shipwreck, one beating with rods and no synagogue whipping. Of course, we cannot know when these things happened, but we can be certain that there were travels, dramatic incidents and maybe some very important stories that were not included in Acts' account of Paul's mission. Now is one time when they may have happened.

Another intriguing event in Paul's life that is not mentioned in Acts happened at this time. While writing to Corinth around AD 56, he tells them of a profound mystical experience and 'extraordinary revelations' that were given him fourteen years previously. He was taken up to the third heaven, into Paradise and heard things that no mortal is permitted to speak. Obviously we do not find out from Paul what he heard (though in 388 a Christian claimed to have found the *Apocalypse of Paul* in the basement of Paul's house in Tarsus, along with his sandals, recounting the rather hair-raising visions), nor does he give us any indication whether the experience had any influence on what he taught or on his mission. What he does tell us of its results is more oblique than ever. 'To keep me from being too elated, a thorn was given me in the flesh, a messenger of Satan to torment me.' This nameless affliction has been variously interpreted as religious persecution, sexual temptation or a physical disorder (with countless suggestions about the latter, from epilepsy to bad hearing). He appealed to the Lord to be delivered from it, but was refused, being told 'Power is made perfect in weakness.'

CHAPTER 11

Spies in Antioch

In AD 47, Paul's Christian faith was about fourteen years old, and the church itself about seventeen. How were things shaping up so far for the new church? As with most questions considered in this book, it is hard to say. Our information is very patchy, and mostly about Paul and Barnabas and the Antioch church, overlooking what had been going on elsewhere.

It seems that opposition to Christianity was as intense as ever. Not only did Paul and Barnabas's mission provoke violence from Jewish locals, but also official harassment in Palestine had either revived or continued unabated. While Acts tell us that the church had peace after the conversion of Paul, that may be less true for Jerusalem than Syria. After all, the defection of a Pharisee who had been attacking Christians abroad for his own pious reasons would make little difference to the hostility of the priestly politicians in Jerusalem.

The first martyr among the apostles was executed on the orders of King Herod some time before his death in AD 44, to bolster his support from their priestly enemies. This was James the brother of John, both of whom had asked Jesus for the two highest positions in his coming kingdom, confident that they could drink that cup that he would drink and be baptized with his baptism. Apart from the fact that he was beheaded, Acts has no details about James's death, which is surprising when one considers how much information it has about Stephen's death a decade earlier – a reminder how much must have happened in the early church that Acts knows nothing about. (Later tradition says that the man who handed James over repented, asked James's forgiveness, and the two of them were executed together.) Acts says that Herod tried to repeat his success by arresting Peter, but that Peter escaped from prison, was rescued by an angel, and fled from Jerusalem. His absence is thought by some to have helped ensure that James, the brother of Jesus, was seen as head of the Jerusalem church.

We know that the faith had spread northwards through Syria from Damascus to Antioch, and into Asia Minor – maybe via Cilicia, but certainly around the regions of southern Galatia. This is all the expansion we know of in the 40s, but there may have been more. We know nothing of the exploits of people that in later years at least seem to have travelled far, such as John, Philip and Peter himself (though there is some evidence that Peter had already reached Rome). Equally we know nothing of the coming of the gospel to certain places that were later to be major centres of Christianity, most notably Alexandria. With its enormous Jewish population about the same distance west of Jerusalem along the African coast as Antioch was to the north, it seems unlikely that Christian mission would long have delayed approaching the city. Unconvincing later tradition connects John Mark with the first church in Alexandria, but who went where when is unknown to us.

However, we glimpse something like the tip of an evangelistic iceberg in a report from the Roman historian Suetonius. He says that the Emperor Claudius expelled all 50,000 Jews from Rome in about AD 49, because they 'constantly made disturbances at the instigation of Chrestus'. Since 'Chrestus' was a possible alternative spelling of the Latin *Christus*, Suetonius is generally thought to be referring to conflict between Christians and non-Christian Jews of the kind that we have seen in Paul's travels. Moreover, Acts tells us that the Christians Priscilla and Aquila had been among the Jews expelled from Rome. If Christianity had indeed already made the 1,500-mile journey to Rome (and we know for sure that it was well established there before Paul wrote about eight years later) then who can guess where else it might have gone?

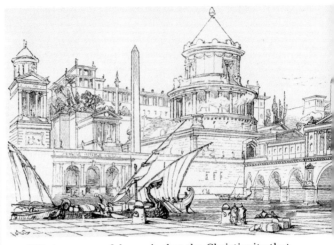

What we can safely say is that the Christianity that was taking root to the north in Syria and Asia Minor was of a significantly different variety from that which predominated in Jerusalem. We should not oversimplify this to a precise equation of Antioch = Greek-speaking = anti-law = mission to Gentiles, while Jerusalem = Aramaic = pro-law = mission to Jews. Doubtless the attitudes in both communities were more complex and subtle than that, and varied from one person to another. Nevertheless, these were the basic lines of difference between the two, a difference that was about to become explosive.

However, as we come to the crisis about circumcision which culminated in the Jerusalem council, so vital to the future of the church, we unfortunately reach the point where it becomes more difficult than anywhere else to unravel the tangled threads of Paul's letters and Acts. In attempts to do so, scholars have placed the event anywhere from before Paul's first missionary journey to towards the end of his travels – not to mention their disagreements over what actually happened at the council. The main question is whether the meeting in Jerusalem that Paul describes in Galatians 2 is the same Jerusalem council recounted in Acts 15. If it is then there are important

contradictions between the two accounts; if not then we run into very serious difficulties with the timing of events.

A strong case can be made for Galatians being written before the Jerusalem council, and therefore describing a different meeting. This would allow us to take Acts' account of the council at face value because Paul makes no reference to the council whatsoever. Unfortunately it would also require Paul's stay in Tarsus (which Acts covers almost in one verse) to last for fourteen years of which we know nothing, and then the whole of Acts 12–18 (including Paul's first two missionary journeys) to squeeze into three years or so, which is incredibly tight. Thus both the weight of scholarship and (marginally) of the evidence support the identification of the Galatians 2 meeting with the Jerusalem council of Acts, and that is the interpretation we shall follow here – and have followed already, in fact, because according to the alternative theory the meeting Paul describes in Galatians happened during his year in Antioch before the first missionary journey.

The crisis was about Gentiles and the law of Moses. It should be clear by now that the policy of Antioch towards Gentiles – allowing them full Christian status without obedience to the Law, and sharing food with them – was by no means the only one possible for the church, nor even the most obviously right. Christianity was nothing more or less than a renewed Judaism, claiming the fulfilment that so many Jews had been waiting for – the messiah, the coming of the Lord, the revival of Israel and the conversion of the Gentiles. While many Christians, in Palestine as well as in Antioch, could make the astonishingly radical leap of accepting that Gentiles could enter this renewed, messianic Judaism without the law of Moses, it is no surprise that some were not so willing.

And so it was that in AD 47, to choose the most likely date, some visitors came from Jerusalem to Antioch. They were some of the more orthodox members of the mother church, certainly a lot more conservative in their attitude to the Law than the radicals of Antioch. They may well, like Paul, have been Pharisees, but unlike him had continued in their absolute devotion to the Law after becoming Christians. Maybe with James now in command, and with renewed assaults from the authorities, the Jerusalem church was becoming more committed to a rigorous devotion to the Law.

We read of this visit in Acts. Paul does not clearly mention such a thing preceding the Jerusalem council, merely saying that he went to Jerusalem 'in response to a revelation', which is intriguing but vague. However, he may be talking about these visitors to Antioch when he refers to 'false believers secretly brought in, who slipped in to spy on the freedom we have in Christ Jesus'.

The men may have been official delegates from the Jerusalem church, sent to report on the religion that was being taught and practised in Antioch in the name of Jesus. It is likely that the Jerusalem church was concerned by what they had been hearing and wanted more information.

If this was indeed their job, they overstepped the mark. Dismayed that Gentiles had been admitted to the church without submitting to the law of Moses, they told them that they needed to be circumcised. Until that happened, they were missing out on a vital and basic part of their new religion. It was wonderful that they had faith in Jesus, but that made little sense if they were not willing to practise the faith *of* Jesus. They would not find acceptance before the God of the Jews until they were circumcised as he had instructed.

Paul versus the circumcisers

'We did not submit to them for a minute,' Paul says. However essential observing the Law was to the Christian gospel in the eyes of the Judean visitors, in Paul's mind it was equally fundamental to the gospel that the Gentiles were free from it.

Although we have little direct information here, we can easily reconstruct his arguments from what he says in Galatians, which deals at length (and in heat) with the same issue a few years later. The law of Moses, Paul argued, had been God's provision for the Jewish people, and their way of being the people of God. Now, however, the gospel of Christ had come, offering something far better, and not just for Jews but for all people. Gentile Christians had received the Spirit of God and union with Christ, therefore dying in him to their sinful flesh and sharing already in his resurrection. Since these were the promised blessings of the age to come, the Gentiles had already in some sense attained in Christ the ultimate goals of the Jewish faith (though they would come to complete fullness only at the coming of the Lord).

In other words, Paul said, in Christ the Gentile Christians had all that the Law could offer (being the people of God) and far more that it never could (the Spirit, union with Christ, resurrection, 'righteousness' before God). And they had received all this without coming under the Law.

So, for one thing, circumcision was pointless, gaining the Gentiles nothing that they did not already have. But Paul went further and argued that it would be positively disastrous. Circumcision meant turning back to an outmoded, pre-Christian way of knowing God and of being his people, turning back from all the new gifts that they had enjoyed through believing in the gospel. They would,

'Paul is the patron saint of thought in Christianity. And all those who think to serve the faith in Jesus by destroying freedom of thought would do well to keep out of his way.'
ALBERT SCHWEITZER

Paul claimed, be turning back from Christ. With an appropriately incisive metaphor he warns the Galatians, 'You who want to be justified by the Law have cut yourselves off from Christ; you have fallen away from grace.'

In fact, Paul presents a shockingly negative view of the law of Moses in Galatians. The Jews before Christ had

Moses Receiving the Tablets of the Law, by Lorenzo Ghiberti, fifteenth century.

been under 'the curse of the Law', 'imprisoned under the Law', 'minors', 'no better than slaves', under the charge of 'weak and beggarly spirits'. He repeatedly associates the Law and its physical rituals with 'the flesh' in opposition to the Spirit, and says of himself, 'I died to the Law, so that I might live to God.'

Two points about this. One is that Paul is writing as a convert himself. It is said – to give a rather down-to-earth analogy – that ex-smokers are often the most ardent anti-smokers. Similarly, since Paul was formerly so passionately and bloodily devoted to the Law, now that he preached Christianity without the Law it is understandable that he might swing to the opposite extreme.

More importantly, Galatians was written in the heat of battle, a battle for the survival of the gospel as Paul saw it, and every word of the letter rings with the clash of swords. In 1934, the theologian Karl Barth, alarmed by a movement he saw as subverting the gospel and playing into the hands of Nazism, published an article entitled simply *No!* This would be a perfect title for Galatians, which is very much in the same spirit. Paul gives the impression of pulling out every stop he can lay his hands on, throwing together every argument and every tactic that will gain him any ground. If we want a calm and balanced exposition of Paul's mature theology of Gentiles and the Law we will have to wait for the book of Romans, but if we want a snapshot of Paul in fighting mood we could not do better. However, this means that Galatians may well present a more extreme position than Paul took at Antioch, showing us the boiling point of a conflict that in AD 47 was just warming up.

The key phrase of all Paul's writings against the circumcisers, however, which doubtless featured in his altercations at Antioch, was 'justification by faith'. This is one that needs a chapter to itself.

Justification by Faith

'A person is justified not by the works of the Law but through faith in Christ,' Paul tells the Galatians, as he will have explained at length when the circumcision issue first arose in Antioch. This is held by many to be the central point of Paul's thought. It is probably the most difficult to grasp and certainly the most controversial.

The phrase has had a long and troubled history since Paul coined it, which we need to consider briefly before we can disentangle Paul's own meaning. One crucial point first. We have two sets of words in English to translate one set of Greek. 'Just' translates the same word as 'righteous'; 'justice' the same word as 'righteousness'. There is unfortunately no verb in the 'righteous' set that is equivalent to 'justify'. Each set has its strengths and weaknesses, so we are forced to cut between the two, but one should bear in mind that the Greek that Paul uses is always the same in each case.

Justification was central to the seminal conflict between Augustine and Pelagius at the start of the fifth century. Pelagius insisted that if God created us and gave us rules to follow, then logically we must be able to follow those rules, and so in our natural strength and by our own God-given free will we can live a life good enough to satisfy God. Augustine argued, on the basis of Paul's teaching, that all humans are broken by the fall, so that no one now can be righteous enough to satisfy God's standards. The idea that we can obey God's law in our natural strength is the 'justification by works of the Law' that Paul says is impossible. Augustine's explanation of how we are instead justified by faith is that those who put their faith in Christ are given grace which heals the soul, giving them a love of righteousness that enables them to keep God's law. This became the official doctrine of Roman Catholicism, although the Eastern church never accepted it.

A millennium later, justification became a hot issue again in the Protestant reformation, Martin Luther attacking Catholic teaching with a radical new interpretation of Paul. Luther had a more pessimistic view of humanity even than Augustine. Experience convinced him that no human could attain the kind of righteousness Augustine described, even with God's help, because God's standard is perfection and no one can be perfect in this life. Luther therefore associated the 'justification by works' opposed by Paul with any hope of satisfying God by the actual holiness of one's life. The righteousness that comes by faith is not a change in behaviour but a change in the way God sees us. He does not enable us actually to attain righteousness, he imputes righteousness to us – he transfers the righteousness of Christ to our account, if you will. He deigns to see us, while we continue to sin, 'clothed in righteousness divine', in Charles Wesley's words. 'Sin is not held against us for Christ's sake,' explained Luther.

Ironically, Luther saw this interpretation of justification by faith as a revival not just of Paul's teaching but of Augustine's. This is true inasmuch as that the Catholic theology he was brought up with had slipped halfway between Pelagius and Augustine, so that Luther was indeed restoring the latter's emphasis on grace and faith, but with a seriously new slant.

The new perspective

Now thanks to Sanders and those who have added to his work in the last thirty years, mainly J.D.G. Dunn and N.T. Wright, we have another radically new interpretation on the table, though often incorporating points made by earlier scholars. Unlike Augustine's and Luther's innovations, it is not likely to change history, but it could make a huge difference to our understanding of Paul's teaching. This 'new perspective', so called, is actually a number of new perspectives as each writer presents different versions. Nevertheless, the most important points are these:

1. Traditional Christian readings of Paul have seriously misrepresented first-century Judaism as a legalistic religion of 'works-righteousness'. In fact, it knew God's grace every bit as much as Christianity. Living by the Law

Paul's letters

Paul wrote letters to his churches as a poor substitute for being there in person. Only after his death did they begin to realize that they had something that would preserve his teaching intact better than word of mouth, by which time some were already lost. There are thirteen letters from Paul in the Bible, though his authorship is questioned in some cases, and others seem to be compilations of more than one letter. The dates are very uncertain.

1 and 2 Thessalonians: To remind a church of the basics of his teaching, and correct their ideas on Christ's second coming.

Galatians: Opposing those who tell Gentiles that they need to be circumcised.

1 Corinthians: Addressing many areas where they have gone off the rails, from personality cults to the resurrection.

2 Corinthians: At least two letters, one calling back those who reject his leadership, another celebrating reconciliation.

Romans: Paul's *magnum opus*, setting out his gospel for an unknown church.

Philippians: Written from prison, rejoicing in the encouraging state of this church.

Colossians and Ephesians: Written from prison, exploring the blessings of Christ for the church. Authorship questioned.

Philemon: A short letter encouraging Philemon to free his runaway slave.

1 and 2 Timothy, Titus: The 'pastoral letters', dealing with church order and sound doctrine. Authorship widely questioned.

was not how one appeased God, but a grateful response to being chosen by him.

2. This makes a great difference to how we understand Paul's 'not works but faith' statements, not least because it follows that Paul is arguing not against standard Jewish ideas of justification, but against misled Christians.

3. The very idea of justification, in Paul and Judaism, is not a matter of individual salvation but a more corporate one of how the people of God are marked out.

4. Dunn and Wright argue that the 'works' that Paul disparages are not 'good works' in the sense of moral living or self-help religion, but the specific demands of the law of Moses, especially those designed to set the Jewish people apart – circumcision, the sabbath, feasts – the 'badges of Judaism'.

5. Dunn and Wright also go further than Sanders in redefining 'righteousness'. Christians since Augustine have understood the term as meaning 'moral perfection' (whether actual or imputed). For Jews such as Paul, it referred instead to fulfilling the terms of a covenant, meeting the obligations of a relationship.

6. Sanders also argues that justification is something of a side issue for Paul, and not the central idea that others have seen it as. He has less support here.

What then did Paul teach his followers about justification in these years of turmoil? Has a coherent new understanding of Paul emerged, or are we faced with more confusing possibilities than ever? A quarter-century is a short time in theology, too soon to judge the success of the 'new perspective', and in fact much of it is a lot more recent. It is far from sweeping all before it, and it is safe to say there are problems with it as well as impressive insights.

'Our beloved brother Paul wrote to you according to the wisdom given him, speaking of this as he does in all his letters. There are some things in them hard to understand, which the ignorant and unstable twist to their own destruction.'

2 PETER 3:15

Nevertheless it seems to me to offer tremendous help in understanding Paul.

To start on the surest ground, when Paul denies 'justification by works', he is not attacking a system where individuals earn personal salvation by their faultless lives. First-century Judaism certainly taught nothing like that, and neither did the Christian circumcisers. When Paul says that we are not justified by the works of the Law, he is talking about circumcision, saying that it adds nothing to Christians' relationship with God and is not necessary to being his people.

The clearest demonstration that the works that Paul is downplaying are circumcision and other such Mosaic rites, rather than living a good life in general, is in the ethical exhortations at the end of Galatians. Having attacked with all his might those who make works essential to salvation, he moves smoothly and seamlessly on to add that living a good life *is* essential to salvation: those who do not 'will not inherit the kingdom of God'. He therefore could not possibly include living a good life in what he means by 'works'. Rather than belonging among works that cannot justify, holy living is an integral part of the faith that does.

That said, one can certainly argue that Augustine's and/or Luther's attacks on self-help moralism were legitimate applications or extensions of Paul's teaching to new situations, but if we want to understand Paul himself, we must remember that he was not denying what they were denying.

So much for unprofitable works. What then is the faith that does justify a person? According to Sanders, the concept is a largely negative one, which seems quite credible. What Paul means when he says that we are justified by faith is, above all, that we are not justified by works. It is another way of saying that circumcision is not necessary.

Nevertheless, if we were to press Paul for a positive explanation of how a person is justified, I think we can piece together a reasonable impression of how he would answer. One believes the gospel and is baptized, thereby receiving the Spirit and being in Christ, dying to the sinful flesh and living as one resurrected with Christ. Something like this seems to lie behind Paul's shorthand 'by faith'.

This brings us to the most crucial question of what Paul means by 'righteousness' and 'justification'. Dunn and Wright agree that when we talk about 'righteousness' in English, we rarely mean what Paul meant. The Western theological concept of 'righteousness' is derived from Greek philosophy, an abstract ideal against which a person's behaviour is measured. The Hebrew scriptures mean something rather different by the term – a more concrete idea about being in a covenant relationship – and Paul uses it in the same way.

However, having agreed about what the Hebrew idea of justification is not, Dunn and Wright do not agree about what it is, so here we are on shakier ground.

For Dunn, on the one hand, it is a relational term. The righteous do what their relationships require of them. The

A Greek papyrus
text of
Romans, from
c. AD 180–200.

righteousness of God is not his moral perfection or his impartial judgment on sin but his faithfulness in doing all that he has promised to his people – which is why it is celebrated rather than feared in the Psalms: 'My mouth will tell of your righteous acts, of your deeds of salvation all day long.' The righteous are those who live as their relationship with God requires. So in justifying sinners, God mends the relationship, faithfully reconciling the unfaithful to himself so that they can now be faithful.

As Dunn notes, if one accepts this understanding then the Protestant–Catholic dispute – whether justification means being made righteous in thought, word and deed (à la Augustine) or reckoned as righteous despite thought, word and deed (à la Luther) – rather disintegrates. When God reckons us as reconciled to him, despite our unfaithfulness, in so doing he effects actual reconciliation. (It has long been argued on other counts that the Protestant–Catholic clash over justification is a dispute about terms between those who largely agree in substance. May the 'new perspective' prove another nail in its coffin.)

The evidence for Dunn's interpretation of righteousness in pre-Pauline texts has left many unconvinced, which is a shame because it has the immeasurable advantage of making perfect sense of everything that Paul says on the subject.

According to Wright, on the other hand, justification is not God's action in bringing people into this covenant relationship, but his declaration about who is in it. The word is very close in meaning to 'vindication'. Israel's great hope from the coming of the Lord was that in front of everyone the judge of the world would prove Israel to be his true people, the righteous. That day of judgment was anticipated here and now by the Law because it too marked off the righteous from the unrighteous, demonstrating who were and were not the true covenant community of God. Paul's argument against justification by works of the Law is that it is no longer circumcision, etc., that mark off the covenant community, but faith in Christ.

When there are such important disagreements as this, we are clearly faced not with one but with several new perspectives on Paul, and so this illumination of his theology still leaves us somewhat in the dark. However, where there is some agreement, these perspectives are compelling: that Paul and his enemies were arguing more about matters of the covenant community than about individual salvation; that the works of the Law Paul disparaged were only circumcision and suchlike badges of Judaism; and that Paul's Semitic concept of righteousness is different from later Christian definitions.

Whatever the uncertainties about Paul's theology, the story of his life is pretty clear at this point. Jewish Christians from Jerusalem tried to persuade the Gentile Christians of Antioch of the necessity of circumcision, while Paul did and said everything in his power to dissuade them.

And despite the problems of interpreting the arguments he used against the circumcisers, we can say with confidence what his fundamental objection was to their teaching, the basic reason for his horror. The heart of the issue for Paul was that the gospel cannot be tied to national identity. Its whole glory was that it was coming out from Israel to all nations, opening the floodgates of God's grace. The Law, however, was fundamentally exclusive, all about being a separate holy nation. Adding such Jewish boundary markers as circumcision to the gospel was, in Paul's eyes, turning it from salvation for all nations to salvation for the Jewish nation and those willing to join it. It was putting the outpouring of God's grace back into the tap.

This point was crucial enough for Paul that the circumcisers were not merely wrong, but teaching a different gospel. And so when argument failed to silence them, the only option was to take the dispute back to Jerusalem, the mother church and the source of the trouble.

The Jerusalem Council

Paul and Barnabas set off with some friends from Antioch for Jerusalem in AD 48. Acts says that they were appointed for the job by the church, while Paul in Galatians (if he is talking about the same meeting) says rather cryptically that they went in response to a revelation. We have already seen how the church appointed Paul and Barnabas as overseas missionaries on the inspiration of the Holy Spirit, and it seems that such charismatic decision-making was behind their visit to Jerusalem as well.

On the way, they took the chance to visit various Christian communities outside Judea, enthusing them with the news of Gentile Christianity. This was good politics, allowing them to claim widespread support for their approach.

Whether Paul was spoiling for a fight with Jerusalem or expecting a friendly meeting of minds would depend on whether he believed the circumcisers were broadcasting the teaching of the Jerusalem church or taking things into their own hands. As it turned out the circumcisers were pretty much on their own, though they are unlikely to have made that entirely clear to the Antiochenes.

Among the friends who accompanied Paul and Barnabas was a convert by the name of Titus. He was a Gentile Christian and uncircumcised, brought to the Jerusalem church as a test case, you might say – or less sympathetically, as a provocative gesture calculated to put the conservatives in an awkward position.

They received a friendly enough welcome from the Jerusalem church, and then settled down to discuss the question that would change the shape of Christianity more than any other in its history: do Gentile Christians need to follow the law of Moses?

The essential outcome of the meeting is clear enough: it was a victory for Paul. Almost everything else about it is unclear, though, because of the intractable problem of whether it is the meeting Paul mentions in Galatians or not. If it is, we must accept Paul's personal recollections

A model of first-century Jerusalem, in the Holy Land Hotel, Jerusalem.

where they differ from Acts, which is often. If not, then Acts is our only source of information, and a substantially different picture emerges.

Assuming it is the same meeting, we must see it as a small private meeting between Paul and Barnabas on the one hand, and James, Peter and John on the other, although Acts gives the impression of a rather larger affair. Paul outlined what he had been teaching the Gentiles, and the apostles listened critically. They also give conflicting evidence about how heated the discussion was – though not in the way one might expect. Luke is often seen, not unfairly, as a harmonizer, smoothing over conflicts in the church, but here it is he who describes a long and fierce debate before Paul is vindicated. One can

see the dramatic value of this. In Paul's account, however, the whole thing is something of an anti-climax: he tells the apostles what he has been preaching; they agree that it is sound; end of debate. Paul, one might think, has his own reasons for stressing the harmony of the occasion – to convince doubters that his gospel has Jerusalem's approval. But since he then goes straight on to describe a later blistering row with Peter over a closely related issue, this motive cannot count for very much. It seems the council was both short and sweet.

The leaders of the Jerusalem church agreed with Paul then: the church had to accept the uncircumcised. It had to offer full membership to Gentiles without expecting them to follow the law of Moses. Titus was not a second-class Christian. As Acts depicts it, Peter vigorously supported Paul from the first because of his own experience among Gentiles, while James took a little longer to come round. This sits well with what we know of them from elsewhere. James being devoted to the law of Moses, he was not naturally inclined to dispense with it for Gentiles, and certainly expected Jews to follow it – unlike Paul and Peter.

James's decree

Where the evidence in Acts and Galatians most seriously diverges is over the conclusion to the council. According to Galatians, having agreed about circumcision, they agreed to a division of labour. Peter would be apostle to the Jews and Paul to the Gentiles. The only other requirement made of Paul was that he organize relief for the poor, which he said he was keen to do.

According to Acts, however, James not only chaired the meeting so that the final verdict was his own rather than merely a consensus, but he also then announced a minimalist version of the law of Moses that the Gentiles should follow:

I have reached the decision that we should not trouble those Gentiles who are turning to God, but we should write to them to abstain only from things polluted by idols and from fornication and from whatever has been strangled and from blood.
ACTS 15:18–19

The first rule seems to prohibit not only idol worship but also eating food that has previously been offered to an idol. Strangled meat was unclean because the law forbade eating anything with blood still in it. The fourth rule seems to duplicate this, unless it is understood as forbidding bloodshed. The point of these rules would seem to be to ask concessions of the Gentiles, so that Jews would have fewer problems of conscience about eating with them – food law, idolatry and sexual ethics being the main issues between Jews and pagans.

The two versions of the council seem quite irreconcilable at this point. Paul explicitly denies that the Jerusalem leaders made any demands of him beyond remembering the poor. Paul's ferocious attitude throughout the whole of Galatians to the idea of Gentiles being asked to obey the Law and to the idea of moderating his stance out of respect for Jerusalem makes it hard to believe that, at the meeting he describes there, he accepted a mini Torah to be imposed on Gentiles.

And even if Acts and Galatians are describing two separate meetings, it still seems surprising that Paul should agree to the decree at any point, considering what we read in his letters. His independence and his insistence that Gentiles are under no law seem to leave little room for adding James's rules to his gospel, and sure enough he never mentions them anywhere in his writings (though there are plenty of other important things he does not mention either).

However, he certainly expects his followers to abstain from fornication and bloodshed. He never mentions strangled meat, but his attitude to meat offered to idols is interesting. He tells the Corinthians that they must not eat at pagan feasts – 'you cannot participate in the table of the Lord and the table of demons'. But as for meat from the market (which was often the gods' leftovers) Paul tells them that they are free to follow their liberal consciences – but only so far as it offends no one else. 'If food is a cause of their falling, I will never eat meat, so that I may not cause one of them to fall.' He takes the same approach in Romans: 'Everything is indeed clean, but it is wrong for you to make others fall by what you eat; it is good not to eat meat or drink wine or do anything that makes your brother or sister stumble.' His policy is that once the fundamental principle is secure (that Gentiles do not have to live by the law of Moses in order to be Christians), practical concessions and restrictions for the sake of others (such as staying kosher in order to eat with law-abiding Jews) are not only acceptable but the true, self-effacing way of Christ.

Seen in this light, it is not inconceivable that if James was willing to concede that the Gentiles are justified without the works of the Law, Paul in return might agree to ask them to abide by James's rules where fellowship with Jews was at stake.

How then should we see this alleged decree? Various

answers have been offered. It could be entirely genuine, or complete fiction. It could be genuine, but developed later than the Jerusalem council and included here either because this is where Luke thought it belonged, or because it came soon after and could therefore be legitimately merged. Or it may indeed have been made by James at the council but then completely ignored by Paul.

Acts 21 is suggestive here. On a visit to Jerusalem a decade later, Paul is told by James (in one of the first-person, 'eye-witness' passages) that the thousands of law-abiding Christians in Jerusalem have heard alarming reports that Paul is persuading even the Jews of the dispersion to neglect the Law. In response, James says, he had written to the Gentiles asking them to follow these four rules – but without any hint that he is repeating himself.

The Holy Spirit

Jews of Paul's day saw the Holy Spirit as a way in which the transcendent God acted in the world. They often talked of the Spirit not just as part of God, but as if he were a distinct individual sent by God – much as Christians talked of Jesus. Paul took this thoroughly on board, seeing the Holy Spirit, like Jesus, both as an agent of God and as intimately identified with the person of God.

But the Spirit was not just like another Christ sent alongside Jesus. For Paul he is not just the Spirit of God but the Spirit of Christ, sent with a distinct mission to inhabit believers and bring the presence of Christ to the Church. It was this demanding threefold vision of God that the church later had to try to unpack in developing the doctrine of the Trinity.

The Holy Spirit has a central and many-sided mission in the life of the church, according to Paul. The Spirit brings new life to those who believe the gospel, and lives in them. He guides, strengthens and helps them grow in the spiritual life. He directs and empowers worship. He inspires prophecy, works miracles and gives many other spiritual gifts. He empowers evangelism and convinces unbelievers. The power and guidance of the Spirit are reasons why Christians need follow neither the law of Moses nor the urges of the flesh. And finally, the Spirit is a down-payment or foretaste of all the joys in store for believers in the age to come.

Adding this piece to the puzzle, it seems unlikely either that Luke has simply dreamed up the decree – twice – or that it was an official resolution of the Jerusalem council subscribed to and broadcast by Paul (and later forgotten by James). It is not impossible that James expressed some similar policy at the conference or that Paul honoured it in his churches. But the formal 'apostolic decree' as Luke knows it is more likely to have developed from the conflict over table fellowship that we come to in the next chapter, combined into one story because they were close together in time.

This is not certain. What is certain, however we read the evidence, is that the Jerusalem leaders heard Paul's version of the gospel, including his insistence that the Gentiles were not subject to the law of Moses, and concurred. In this, the Jerusalem council was one of the greatest turning points in the history of the church.

In agreeing with the missionaries to the Gentiles that converts did not need circumcision, the Jerusalem leaders were throwing the doors of the church open. Christianity was no longer just another sect of Judaism but a world religion in embryo, combining the compelling Jewish world view with universal access. Whereas mainstream Judaism was based on racial exclusiveness, the council of Jerusalem turned Christianity into a faith for all nations and made it fundamentally adaptable. As a result, the church would grow phenomenally for centuries, but within just one century it became predominantly Gentile. Another 150 years and it was banning eating with Jews. Four centuries after the death of Jesus, it was pursuing violent persecution of Jews.

If Paul and Barnabas had not succeeded in winning general acceptance for their inclusive policy, the Christian faith as we know it would not exist – but there has been a steep price to pay.

C H A P T E R   1 4

More Troubles, More Travels

P aul and Barnabas returned from Jerusalem to
Antioch with the news of their success – not so
much that the verdict of Jerusalem had gone their
way, but rather that they had convinced their brothers
and sisters of the truth. Two Jerusalem prophets, Judas
and Silas, accompanied them, sent by James to assure
doubters that he had indeed decided against circumcision.
They stayed there a while, and Silas became a close friend
of Paul's.

After a while, another visitor arrived in Antioch: Peter.
He, as we have seen, was not a stickler for the Law. Quite
happy with the idea of welcoming the uncircumcised into
the church, he was doubtless keen to see the long-awaited
harvest of the Gentiles and to play his part alongside Paul
and Barnabas – apostle to the Jews or not.

Many eyes were on Peter, to see whether he would eat
with Gentiles. It was one thing allowing them to escape
circumcision, but would the great man compromise his
own obedience to the Law by eating with them? Paul and
Barnabas did, certainly – and took a relaxed attitude to
other regulations too – but for many Antioch Jews this was
going too far, and they looked to the Jerusalem apostle to
show some rigorous discipleship and orthodox leadership.

In fact, Peter lived like Paul and Barnabas, to the
disappointment of conservatives. They complained to
James: Christianity was turning into an apostate sect for
Jews who didn't want to be Jews any more. James was
unhappy too and sent a team to investigate. They told
Peter that it was a disgrace for Jews to abandon the Law –

whatever Gentiles did. He ought to live as a proper Jew and stop eating with the uncircumcised as the Law demanded.

Peter was in an invidious position. He was acting on the personal conviction that as a Christian Jew he was free from the Law, and more importantly acting in solidarity with the Gentiles. They were united in following Jesus and should not be divided by ritual. If the God of Israel had accepted them as they were, it could not be right for his fellow Christians to turn them away from their tables.

And yet the issue was such a fiery one for the conservatives that it looked as if it would split the church. They had already swallowed a bitter draft in accepting – those who had accepted it – that Gentiles did not need to submit to the law of Moses to be considered Christians, but this was too much. And since they had conceded the fundamental point, was it not in order for the triumphant radicals of Antioch to make a concession themselves – to stop eating with the uncircumcised for the sake of the unity of the church?

This is precisely what Peter did, and others followed his lead – most notably Barnabas. From now on, circumcised and uncircumcised would worship together the same Lord but would not share the same bread or drink from the same cup.

Paul went apoplectic. He confronted Peter face to face and accused him of hypocrisy, of not living by the truth of the gospel. 'If you, though a Jew, live like a Gentile and not like a Jew, how can you compel the Gentiles to live like Jews?' Of course, Peter was not directly forcing anyone to do anything. But he was putting Gentile Christians in a position where they either had to accept second-class status or submit to the law of Moses after all. The problem was not that Peter was following the Law for the sake of show. Paul insists throughout his letters that he is the first one to accept unnecessary prohibitions when it helps people to embrace the gospel. But this was

'I suspect that were Paul to visit us today, he would still be a social outcast and a deviant, still be seen as a fanatic even in many conservative religious circles. Prophetic figures tend to be heroes only long after they are dead.'

BEN WITHERINGTON, III

the opposite – putting obstacles between Gentiles and the gospel, renewing the barriers between races.

Paul did not win this fight, or certainly not as decisively as the Jerusalem council. He says nothing of the outcome in his account, except that he stuck to his guns, and such diffidence would be very surprising if it had been in his favour. Peter and Barnabas continued trying to unite the church by no longer eating with the uncircumcised, and Paul continued to eat with everybody.

This may be the point when James issued his decree telling the Gentiles to avoid strangled or idolatrous meat, etc. If so, it seems a fair answer to the problem, expecting compromises from each side: Jews in their standards of purity and Gentiles in their lifestyle. The fact that Luke knows the decree so well shows that it was taken on board by some churches at least, but Paul was not a compromiser and does not seem to have been able to accept it.

Back to Galatia

With this kind of atmosphere in Antioch, it is not surprising that Paul began to discuss another missionary trip with Barnabas. They could revisit the new churches, and then go further west.

There was already tension enough between them to make for a difficult trip, but then Barnabas suggested taking his cousin John Mark with them again. Paul would not trust him after his desertion last time. Barnabas resented that and perhaps argued that love always trusts and keeps no record of wrongs. They quarrelled sharply, and in the end decided to go their separate ways. Barnabas and John Mark went back to Cyprus; Paul took the land route into Asia Minor. Instead of Barnabas, he went with his new friend from Jerusalem, Silas.

Paul and Silas crossed Paul's Cilician homeland, possibly visiting churches that he had established there before coming to Antioch. They then went into Galatia, staying again with the Christians in Lystra, Derbe, Iconium and Pisidian Antioch.

In Lystra, another evangelist joined Paul's expedition, a young man called Timothy. Acts makes the most astonishing claim that Paul circumcised him. His mother was Jewish, his father a Gentile, and Luke tells us that Paul was persuaded 'because of the Jews of that place'. Naturally those who are generally suspicious of Acts reject this out of hand on the ground that Paul, the author of Galatians, the ferocious opponent of Gentile circumcision, could not possibly have done such a thing. It is indeed incredible, but there are also problems in discounting the incident. Luke has only just described the Jerusalem council at considerable length, making it the centrepiece of his book, so there is no way he could be oblivious to the oddity of Timothy's circumcision. This makes it unthinkable that Luke could have invented the incident and unlikely that he would accept the story unless it was from a trusted source. Timothy's position as an uncircumcised half-Jew among Jews was somewhat different to that of the Gentiles of Antioch who thought that they could not be Christians without circumcision. Paul's behaviour, as Acts describes it, is unpredictable and not obviously consistent, but only incredible for those who believe people do not do unpredictable and inconsistent things. We have more reason to accept the story than reject it.

'We' come to Europe

Next Paul wanted to tour the province of Asia, the richest in the empire, which dominated the west of Asia Minor. He especially wanted to visit the capital city, Ephesus, but his plans changed.

Acts talks mysteriously at this point about the Holy Spirit forbidding him to preach in Asia, and about Paul deciding therefore to head north into Bithynia and again being prevented by the Spirit of Jesus. So Paul and Silas travelled a couple of hundred miles to the north-western seaport of Troas, which sits across the Aegean from Macedonia. (The Roman province of Macedonia contained much that is now northern Greece as well as modern Macedonia and Albania. The province of Achaia covered southern Greece.) In Troas, Paul had a dream of a man saying, 'Come over to Macedonia and help us,' and so they set sail on a swift two-day journey to Neapolis in the north-east corner of Macedonia. Bearing in mind that they

Paul's travels with Silas, AD 49–50.

had already travelled so far to get to the port, this was
presumably a vision for confirmation or fine-tuning of
Paul's plans.

It was a landmark sea journey for two reasons. It was
Paul's first time in Europe, and although it was not the first
time the gospel had come to Europe, as Christians had

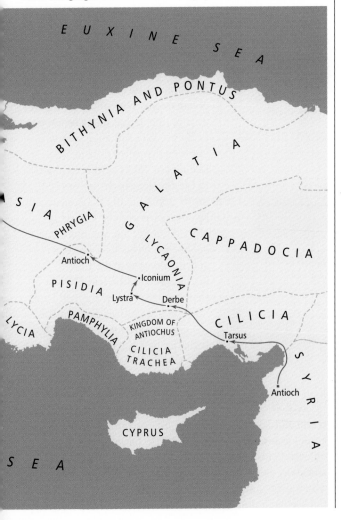

already gone to Rome, it is the first time the narrative of the Bible ever sets foot in Europe.

It is also where the first of Acts' much-debated 'we-passages' starts. In 16:8 we are told, 'they went down to Troas', but then, after Paul's dream, 16:10 says, 'we immediately tried to cross over to Macedonia'. Later 'we' passages include Paul's final visit to Jerusalem and his journey in chains to Rome. What are we to make of them? The traditional and most obvious explanation is that the

author of Acts was a travelling companion of Paul who at these points includes his own recollections. The problem with this assumption is that many see Acts as the work of someone who only knew Paul at second hand. The likeness of Paul's sermons in Acts to the theology of his letters is pretty approximate; there seem to be large gaps in Acts' knowledge of Paul's story; and the more one doubts events such as James's apostolic decree and Paul's broadcasting it, the less likely it is that the writer knew the real Paul.

The alternatives are that the we-passages are lifted more or less verbatim by Luke from an earlier travelogue by a friend of Paul, or that he composed them himself despite not having been present.

Roman fresco of a cargo ship, from first-century Pompeii.

As for the first, on the one hand it seems unlike Luke to use a source so crudely. While his gospel draws very heavily on Mark, for example, and follows it closely, he rewords almost every verse for clarity and style, so it seems strange that he would not bother with a little simple rewording here. If, on the other hand, the 'we' is fictitious, it is fraudulent, because there is little evidence for the claim that this was an accepted stylistic device. That being the case, it is an odd way of glamorizing oneself. The we-passages are often somewhat mundane – focusing on travel arrangements, for example – and this first one gives the impression that, having accompanied Paul and Silas to Philippi, the writer then left them as soon as they got into trouble with the authorities – surely a counterproductive way of impressing one's readers.

Seen in this light, the idea that Acts was written by a person who had travelled a little with Paul – without necessarily becoming an expert in his theology or privy to exhaustive biographical revelations – is harder to discount.

Philippi: demons and prison

Ten miles inland in Macedonia, Paul and his growing band of friends came to the Roman colony of Philippi. It was founded as a new home for the soldiers of Antony and Octavian after their victory there in 42 BC, and the Philippians remained proudly loyal to Rome. On the sabbath, as usual, the missionaries joined the local Jewish worship. It seems there was no synagogue, because Philippi lacked the requisite ten Jewish men, but a group of women met at the river to recite the synagogue prayers and readings (Jewish worship being quite fashionable among women of a certain class) and here the missionaries joined them. Paul told them that the Jewish hope was fulfilled and transformed in the executed and resurrected messiah.

One person at least was convinced, Lydia, a trader in purple dye which she imported from her home city of Thyatira in the province of Asia. She was baptized – perhaps in the river – along with the rest of her household. She pressed the missionaries to leave their paid lodgings and stay with her for as long as they were in town. It was not Paul's policy to accept free board from his converts, preferring to pay his own way and earn his keep, 'that I may make the gospel free of charge'. Consequently,

'He, when among you, accurately and steadfastly taught the word of truth in the presence of those who were then alive.'

POLYCARP, SECOND
CENTURY, TO
PHILIPPI

while he was glad of houses such as Lydia's where he could live and work, he 'did not eat anyone's bread without paying for it'. He preached the gospel at and from Lydia's house for the rest of his stay.

The Christians were on their way to the river on another sabbath when they made a less welcome female acquaintance. This was a slave who made money – for her owners – by telling fortunes. In the pagan world view, this meant she had a python spirit; in the Christian, it meant that she was controlled by an evil spirit. So powerful was her gift that she realized Paul and his friends were Christian preachers, and so she took to following them around, crying, 'These men are slaves of the Most High God, who proclaim to you a way of salvation.' Paul did not believe that all publicity is good publicity, and so he exorcized her.

This enraged her masters, who dragged Paul and Silas off to the praetors, the two city magistrates. According to Acts, the charge was not the violation of property and the ruin of their business, but that 'These men are disturbing our city; they are Jews and are advocating customs that are not lawful for us as Romans to adopt or observe.'

Converting people to Judaism – whichever branch of it – was not illegal, unless one advocated beliefs and practices subversive to Roman order. You could well argue that Paul's teaching did. His later letter to the Philippian church (Philippians 2:9–11) is certainly subversive, insisting that Christian allegiance is to the empire of heaven rather than Rome; and that Jesus, not Claudius, is the true authority over all people. While the oracular entrepreneurs that Paul and Silas had offended may possibly have picked up on such subtexts in their message, their argument before the praetors was more probably simple anti-Semitism. These Jews were fishing for converts in a proud Roman colony where Judaism was quite alien – such an accusation got local observers more worked up than a straightforward loss-of-earnings claim, and so the praetors were persuaded to have Paul and Silas stripped, beaten with rods, and thrown in the inner cells reserved for dangerous low-class

Archaeological remains in Philippi.

criminals, to be expelled from the city in the morning. They were placed in stocks, which may have been an instrument of torture as well as security.

Earthquakes were common enough in the region, and one struck during the night. Acts tells us that Paul and Silas were singing hymns at the time, that the quake shook the foundations, opened the doors and broke all the inmates' chains. When the prison guard came on the scene he was about to kill himself in preference to the punishment for losing his charges, when Paul called out that they were still there.

The details of this story are questioned, not unreasonably. How likely is it, it is said, that an earthquake would release every prisoner from their chains and open the doors, without killing anyone? And if it did happen, how likely is it that they would stay there? And how likely is a prison guard to kill himself without finding out whether his chained prisoners – or their bodies – were still there? We may note that the eye-witness of the earlier verses is no longer present. That said, there is no positive evidence to contradict Luke's story, and we know too little about Roman imprisonment to dismiss it confidently. We are left to decide whether what we know of Luke's reliability gives us reason to trust an otherwise unlikely story.

The Philippian guard asks Paul 'What must I do to be saved?'

The prison guard, with his life in the balance now that Paul's god has come to his rescue, asks, 'What must I do to be saved?' For Paul the question means something a little different. 'Believe in the Lord Jesus, and you will be saved,' he says, 'you and your household.' When the household was gathered, he explained the gospel to them and they were all baptized, adding a new family to the Philippian church.

Household baptism

Twice in Acts, Paul baptizes entire households, those of
Lydia and the Philippian prison guard. This raises some
tricky questions. Ancient households were large. Did Paul
baptize children? Were slaves and wives considered
Christians just because their masters or husbands were?

If Acts is right, Paul's baptisms were less individual
than modern ones, and he did not look too closely at the
personal commitment of junior members. However, his
letters discuss what to do if one's spouse, master or slave
is not a believer, so clearly people also joined the church
on an individual basis too.

In the morning, the praetors sent word to the prison
guard to release Paul and Silas so that they could leave the
city. But Paul would not be got rid of so easily. Protesting
that he and Silas had been subjected, publicly and untried,
to a punishment that it was illegal to inflict on Roman
citizens – which, he announced, they both were – he
demanded that they be honourably escorted away.
Understandably, the officials were alarmed at the news
and did what he said. Less understandable is why Paul
should leave it until now to play his Roman citizen card
rather than before his beating. Could it be that Paul
considered it good for the broadcasting of the gospel
that he suffer public humiliation and then be publicly
vindicated – following the pattern of Jesus, maybe? Or that
as a Christian leader he was unwilling to use personal
privilege to escape afflictions that he expected his flock
to bear bravely – but was willing to make this fact known
afterwards? We can only guess, but it is worth noting that
when he twice refers to this and other such incidents in
2 Corinthians it is a proud boast, his badge as a minister
of Christ.

CHAPTER 15

An Offence to Jews and Foolishness to Greeks

Thessalonica was a thriving port about seventy-five miles from Philippi along the Egnatian Way, and the most important city in Macedonia. This was the next major stop of which Acts has any information.

Paul, Silas and Timothy stayed there a while, working full time both to support themselves and to make contacts among the Gentiles, as well as preaching in the synagogue. Acts says they went there three times for the sabbath meeting, and converted many of the Gentile God-fearers who worshipped there, and a few of the Jews themselves.

Once again, as in Asia Minor, the Jews who did not accept Christianity turned violent – predictably enough for Paul to have warned his converts about it beforehand. They led a riot against the missionaries, attacking the house where they were staying. When they found them away from home they dragged their host, a man called Jason, before the officials. As in Philippi, the charge was a political one – subverting Roman rule, 'saying that there is another king named Jesus'. It would be easy to interpret the charge as deliberately misrepresenting Paul's purely religious teaching as a call to political insurrection, but this would be to misunderstand Paul as well. The division between the religious and political is a modern one that would make little sense to Paul. For him Christianity was an allegiance to the Lord messiah, which cut across all other duties and loyalties, and so was every bit as political as it was religious. Paul was not inciting armed revolt, but he was, in his own way, preaching revolution. Nevertheless, the authorities saw little enough threat in Paul's hosts that they released them on bail, and so Paul, Silas and Timothy left them in peace, leaving that night and heading inland for Berea.

Again, Acts' account of Paul's work in Thessalonica is widely questioned. His letters make it clear that he spent longer there than the three weeks that Acts implies. More importantly the people Paul writes to in 1 and 2 Thessalonians are Gentiles, converted directly from paganism (they 'turned to God from idols' when Paul was there), but Acts talks only of Paul preaching in the synagogue. In Acts, he wins converts by relating scriptural prophecies to the death and resurrection of Jesus, but the letters are uncharacteristically bare of biblical allusion, as if his readers are unfamiliar with the Bible.

It is fairer, though, to say that the letters add to what we read in Acts, rather than discrediting it. Acts does not deny that Paul evangelized the Gentiles as he worked there, it just focuses on his visits to the synagogue, which is sensible enough when it was these that provoked the violence against him, especially if no information about his other activity was available. Even in the synagogue, Acts says, Paul's converts were largely God-fearing Gentiles, so add to this the other pagan converts and it is hardly surprising that the church Paul wrote to was predominantly Gentile. Very little can be made of the lack of biblical references in the letters. Galatians was certainly written entirely to Gentiles, who 'formerly did not know God', and it is smothered in scriptural exposition, so there is little reason to assume that here

A Jewish
limestone tablet
from the fifth
century. Its
purpose was to
give protection
against demons.

Paul is going easy on those who do not know their Bible.

At first the missionaries got a more positive response in Berea. A good number of Gentiles, mostly women, including some of the upper classes, believed what the missionaries preached, and the Jews were open-minded, studying the scriptures to see whether they bore out what Paul was saying, many finding that they did. But trouble started when, following the same pattern as in Galatia, news reached the Thessalonian synagogue that Paul was winning converts in Berea. They came over and denounced Paul effectively enough for violence to flare up again.

The way the Christians handled the situation may offer an intriguing glimpse into the life of Paul. Of the three missionaries, they sent Paul off by sea to Athens while the other two remained to look after the fledgling church. So all three were preachers and leaders, but Paul was the only one it was necessary to get rid of to defuse the situation. He was, it seems, trouble.

Athens: scorned by philosophers

Athens was a city with a past. In earlier centuries it had been the cultural centre of the world, the fount of democracy and philosophy. The university of Plato lived on, but the influence of Athens was greatly diminished. Traditional religion was very much alive, however. Paul took in the splendid temples and shrines of the city, as so many later tourists have done, but where we might see the grand, glorious art and architecture of a quaint, long-dead religion, Paul saw the working machinery of the worship of false gods, which blinded and starved the souls of pagans.

So just as Socrates had done 450 years previously, he took his place in the marketplace and disputed with all comers, arguing for the Jewish belief in one God, creator and judge, against this polytheistic idolatry, and telling them about the coming of Jesus and his resurrection. Acts particularly mentions that he debated with Stoics and Epicureans, whom we met in Chapter 1.

His teaching did not greatly impress the Athenians.

They were immensely proud of their gods and philosophers. Paul's god was not only alien to their ancient pantheon, but rather than offering to slot in quietly he seemed to be making a hostile takeover bid. Moreover, all Greek philosophers, whatever their differences, agreed that the goal of humanity was to escape the material world and the body, whereas the ultimate prize offered by Paul was resurrection, the return of the soul to the body on earth. It is hard to think of a single idea that could be more obviously misguided to the Greek mind. He was 180° wide of the mark. He faced the same response as a fervent teenager correcting a panel of bishops on their theology, ranging from polite amusement to indignation. They dismissed him as *spermologos*, Acts reports, a slang term hard to translate, though 'a pedlar of semi-digested second-hand teaching' gives something of the idea. 'He seems to be a proclaimer of foreign divinities,' they said, which indeed he was, although Acts implies that they may have thought Jesus and Anastasis (Greek for 'resurrection') were his god and goddess.

In the end he was taken to the Areopagus to explain himself. The Areopagus was the supreme court of Athens, though Paul was probably neither being formally tried nor simply being invited to preach, but rather being asked to demonstrate his teaching publicly before some of the leading citizens so that they could weigh up whether it contained anything seditious or worth learning from.

And so Paul delivered his most celebrated sermon in the book of Acts, the arena for another great conflict between Luke and the New Testament scholars. His sermon picks up on the presence in Athens, among numberless shrines, of one 'To an unknown god'. Paul takes this insurance policy as an admission of ignorance, and declares, 'What therefore you worship as unknown, this I proclaim to you'. He starts off with what some of his hearers already know about God: he created, orders and sustains all things, so he can be known and followed by his creatures. But therefore, Paul argues, the worship of idols

'No violence had been offered him in Athens, but the polite amusement which had greeted his witness there was perhaps more difficult to take than violence.'

F.F. BRUCE

and shrines is an insulting nonsense and must be
abandoned. Many Epicureans in particular would agree
with this point, but none with what comes next. Paul
warns that all humanity will be judged by Jesus, a fact
proved by his resurrection from the dead. Sure enough
it is at this point, Luke says, that he lost many of his
listeners, although some came back for more, and a few
were converted. (Even this small success is challenged by
Paul's statement that members of Stephanas's household

An aerial view of
the Acropolis at
Athens.

in Corinth, his next port of call, were his first converts in Greece.)

The scholarly objection to this account is that the sermon is clean contrary to what Paul says on the subject of paganism in his letters, specifically in Romans 1 and 2. In Romans, Paul paints a devastating portrait of humankind without the gospel – deceived, depraved and damned. Here, in contrast, he suggests that all have a natural knowledge of God that comes to fulfilment in Christ. Therefore, it is said, the Areopagus speech in Acts reflects much later Greek-friendly developments in Christian teaching.

The speech is undoubtedly a miniature masterpiece, but is it a historical fiction? A number of things need to be considered here. One is that Paul is by no means a systematic theologian with pat answers to every conceivable question up his sleeve, so it is a mistake to assume that the attitude that he took to the idea of pagans knowing God when he was in an Athenian court before Gentile philosophy-lovers must be identical to the attitude he took eight years later in a letter to Christians and Jews in Rome.

Secondly, the conflict between the two passages depends very much on how they are interpreted. Alternatively, one can argue that the Areopagus speech is a wholehearted attack on paganism where the only real truth Paul concedes they know is that of their own ignorance. And, conversely, Romans 1 and 2 can be read as espousing the very same 'natural theology' that we supposedly find in Acts 17. Paul talks of God being 'seen and understood' by all people, and of pagans being justified on the day of judgment by their obedience to their own conscience. What is more, his attack on paganism at the start of Romans is actually rather an ironic one, designed primarily to trap his readers into seeing the self-condemning hypocrisy of Judaism's judgmentalism towards Gentiles. Bearing these points in mind, the conflict between Acts and Romans seems to be somewhat overstated.

Paul's Christ

When, 250 years later, the church councils started their great debates over who Christ is, they had plenty of material from Paul, but a hard job working it into a systematic creed. He was not inconsistent, but his language was more colourful and poetic than the creeds.

Being Jewish, Paul's starting point is that God is one. But first-century Jews describing God's actions on earth, to preserve his transcendence, talked of their being done by his spirit, word, wisdom, etc. '[Wisdom] brought them over the Red Sea... but she drowned their enemies.'

Paul uses the same approach to talk about 'Christ... the wisdom of God'. It allows him to see Christ not just as a man sent by God but as divine – not another god, but someone intimately identified with the person of God.

Paul's most detailed exploration of Christ's nature is in Colossians, assuming he wrote it. He is the image of God and all God's fullness lives in him. The universe was created through and for him and will be reconciled to him.

This brings into focus the exalted vision of Christ that we catch glimpses of throughout Paul's letters. In Philippians, he talks of Jesus being in the form of God and equal with him. He constantly applies language to him traditionally reserved for God, such as renaming the day of the Lord 'the day of Christ'. Most explicitly, depending on one's translation, he talks in Romans of 'the Messiah, who is over all, God blessed forever'.

Then again, we need to ask what degree of accuracy we should expect from such an account anyway. Neither the writer nor any of Paul's travelling companions was present, apparently. It is possible that the account is based in one way or another on the recollections of an Athenian who became a Christian, or of Paul himself, in which case one would expect it to recall Paul's main drift fairly well, though of course filtered through the memory and interpretation of both the witness and Luke. Alternatively, it is equally possible that Luke constructed the speech himself from what he believed Paul would say in such circumstances. This was entirely proper procedure for first-century historians, but it means the passage tells us less than we would like about what Paul actually said in Athens. If Luke was a genuine travelling companion of Paul we could expect this to be a reasonably good estimate of what he would have said, whereas if he was simply a later admirer who never met him or read his letters, we can expect much less. The reliability of today's scholarly estimates of what Paul could and could not have said in Athens also suffers from the lack of any evidence from his addressing a similar audience.

Paul desperately wanted to return to Thessalonica and revisit the fledgling church, but everything he heard from there confirmed that it was not yet safe and his presence would only stir up worse trouble than they were already facing. Silas and Timothy joined him soon enough in Athens, but they sent Timothy back to Thessalonica to work with the church and encourage them to hold fast. Paul and Silas crossed the isthmus to Corinth to found what was perhaps Paul's most successful and certainly his most troublesome church.

CHAPTER 16

Corinth

The city of Corinth, where Paul and Silas arrived around Easter in AD 50, the twentieth birthday of the church, was only fifty miles over land from Athens, but could hardly have been more different. This was a wealthy, heaving metropolis, offering every kind of entertainment and famed above all for sexual licence. Just as the word 'to welsh' has traditionally reflected the prejudice of English people against their neighbours, so in the ancient world 'korinthiazesthai', 'to do a Corinthian', meant 'to fornicate'. There were theatre and athletic games, thriving trade and tourism, and the great temple of Aphrodite was served by a thousand prostitutes. In coming here from Athens, we are moving, in British terms, from Oxford to Soho.

Paul decided to take a very different approach in Corinth to what we saw in Athens. Having tried to meet the philosophers there on their own terms (without, he may have felt, any great success), he saw that something different was called for here. As he later recalled:

The canal at
Corinth.

*When I came to you, brothers and sisters, I did not come
proclaiming the mystery of God to you in lofty words or
wisdom. For I decided to know nothing among you except
Jesus Christ, and him crucified. And I came to you in
weakness and in fear and in much trembling. My speech and
my proclamation were not with plausible words of wisdom,
but with a demonstration of the Spirit and of power, so that
your faith might rest not on human wisdom but on the
power of God.*

1 CORINTHIANS 2:1–5

It sounds as if he came in a frail and troubled state of
mind, something Acts gives us no hint of. This may have
been because of his failure before the philosophers of
Athens, but equally it may have been from a cause we
know nothing about. Either way, Paul got probably his
most positive response to the gospel yet in Corinth, and
he stayed there for eighteen months.

He quickly became firm friends with a Jewish Christian
couple from Rome called Priscilla and Aquilla. Aquilla, the
husband, was – like Paul – a travelling tentmaker, though
wealthier. They had a house in Ephesus and perhaps
another in Rome, where the church in each place met for
worship. They had recently had to leave Rome after the
clashes between Christians and mainstream Jews became
so unstoppably disruptive that Emperor Claudius expelled
all Jews from the city. Such conflict was evidently not solely
dependent on the presence of Paul.

Both Priscilla and Aquilla were Christian leaders, and
now joined forces with Paul. The fact that, unusually,
Priscilla is more often than not named before her husband
implies that she was the senior and more successful
preacher. They had probably already heard of Paul before
he arrived, because he was now finding that news of his
evangelistic successes was causing a stir throughout the
Christian world.

Following a familiar pattern, Paul and his friends
preached in the synagogue arguing that Jesus was the

messiah, until antagonism forced Paul to give up and stick to his marketplace evangelism. However, the leader of the synagogue, Crispus, was converted and baptized along with his household by Paul, and this made things a lot easier for Paul. There is no record of any violence against him in Corinth, for once, and this is presumably why he was able to stay so long. By the end of Paul's stay another man, Sosthenes, is named as the leader of the synagogue, so it may be that Crispus was forced to step down.

The gospel according to Paul

The key to Paul's gospel is his favourite phrase, recurring ninety times in thirteen letters: 'in Christ'. As William Barclay says, 'It is the summary of his whole religion.' Those baptized into Christ's church enjoy a mystical union with him. This is why his death and resurrection make a difference to us. Jesus' death is not just a sacrifice to atone for our sins – though Paul uses that imagery too – but something that we participate in, crucifying our old sinful selves. In the same way, we will participate in his resurrection, rising to life at his second coming, and in a sense we already do this now through living a renewed life in him.

How does this union work? We cannot push Paul far on soteriological mechanics, but the basic answer is in two ways. Firstly, Christ took human flesh so that just as humanity shares the

corruption of our relative Adam, so we share the wholeness and grace of our relative Jesus. Secondly, Christians receive the Holy Spirit, the Spirit of Christ, which unites us with him and works to transform us into his image.

This salvation is not personal, for Paul, but cosmic. All creation was made through Christ, and all will be restored in him.

Letters to Thessalonica

Presently Timothy arrived from Thessalonica and his report was good. Paul was delighted to hear that the

The ruins of the temple of Apollos in Corinth.

Christians there were standing firm despite continued troubles and that their community was a model of brotherly love.

However, there was one issue where the Thessalonians needed some straightening out. In the few months since Paul had left them, some of the Christians there had died. This threw the church into pitiful confusion. Paul had not promised them that Christians would never die – in fact he assured them that they would share the persecution that had already claimed the lives of believers in Palestine. But he had promised them the imminent return of Jesus, to establish his kingdom in which they would live and rule forever. What then of those who died too soon? Would they not miss the great and glorious day of the Lord?

The issue was hardly a great problem for Paul's theology. The answer was simple and basic: the resurrection of the dead. This hope, that the dead would rise and be vindicated, was one of the main reasons Christians were waiting for the coming of Jesus, so the fact that some Christians were dead hardly undermined that hope. However, Timothy had not known quite what to say to put their minds at rest, and so Paul wrote them a short letter, telling them how pleased he was with them in general and addressing this problem in particular.

He explained that when Jesus returns, all his followers who have died will rise again. They will come to earth with him, and far from missing out will, if anything, meet him before the living.

Death for the Christian, Paul says, is merely to sleep, waking on the day of the Lord to a new life on earth. This was radically different to any view of death that the Thessalonians might have been used to. Some Greek thinkers said that death was extinction; others that it was the liberation of the rational soul from this wayward body, devoutly to be wished. The traditional idea that souls survived in a murky, rather miserable half-life was still

'He was an apostle who was always clear how far he came short of the cause of Jesus Christ himself, without ever falling victim to despair or resignation, or ever giving up hope.'

HANS KÜNG

very popular, but no one imagined the condition was temporary. This is why the Thessalonians had trouble taking on board such a central concept in Paul's teaching, and why even Timothy had not been able to set them straight.

It was a small problem, perhaps, and easily solved. And yet it was hugely significant for the future, because this is our first glimpse of one of the problems that was to dominate the early centuries of the church: how hard it was for Greeks to understand and accept the alien Jewish ideas underlying Christianity. On the one hand, as the church became more and more Gentile, its leaders had to battle against deviant versions of the faith that thrived because they had appealed more to the Greek mindset, while on the other hand the mainstream church itself ended up incorporating Greek ideas that had no support in the Jewish Christianity of Jesus and Paul, such as the immortality of the soul.

This, then, is the background to the letter we know as 1 Thessalonians. The story behind 2 Thessalonians is far less clear. It bears a very close similarity to 1 Thessalonians, the one significant difference being that the error it aims to correct about the second coming of Jesus is that it has already happened. The church has been told, 'either by spirit or by word or by letter', that this is Paul's teaching. He now sets them right by reminding them of the prophetic scenario he had already passed on to them, that before that coming, a man of lawlessness would appear to them, opposing God, doing miracles and setting himself up in the Jerusalem temple.

There are three theories about 2 Thessalonians. The first is that Paul may have written it from Corinth shortly after 1 Thessalonians on hearing of this new problem. The second is that he wrote it shortly before. There is no indication in the letters themselves of which came first (their numbering in the Bible is determined solely by their length), but their similarity suggests they arise from substantially the same situation. The third

theory is that the letter is a forgery, deliberately
modelled on 1 Thessalonians but written decades later
after an idea started circulating that Jesus had returned
spiritually and that this was the only coming to be
expected. The evidence for this is the similarity between
the letters and the insistence of the writer
that it really is from Paul, two facts that
could be explained as the self-authentication
of a forger. However, they could be explained
equally well by the letter indeed having been
written by Paul, so there is no compelling
reason to doubt it.

Paul's eighteen-month stay allowed him
to get to know the Corinthians better than
any other Christians outside Antioch. It could
not last forever, though, and in late AD 51
Paul moved in after another run-in with the
law. He was brought before the new proconsul
of the province, Gallio, the brother of the
Stoic philosopher Seneca, by a delegation led
by Sosthenes the synagogue leader. They
charged him with promoting illegal religious
practices, but Gallio threw the case out. Paul
had committed no offence under Roman law,
he said, and if he had broken the Jewish law,
that was no business of Rome's. Sosthenes
was then mobbed – precisely why or by whom
is not clear – and beaten up in the marketplace, while
the proconsul continued to exercise his neutrality in
Jewish affairs. Soon afterwards, Paul left Corinth to
return home to Antioch.

Historians are grateful for Paul's run-in with Gallio,
because it gives us almost our only fixed date in Paul's
life. An inscription in Delphi dates Gallio's period of office to
the time of Claudius's twenty-sixth acclamation as emperor,
so it would have run from July 51 to June 52. Paul's trial
happened during that time, presumably near the start. Most
other dates in Paul's life are worked out from this point.

Paul sailed with Priscilla and Aquilla as far as Ephesus. This was the great city of the province of Asia that he had tried to reach before and failed, and even now he could spare only a frustratingly short time there. He stayed long enough to visit the synagogue and debate

theology, and this went down well enough for him to be asked to stay. Paul hoped to be back, but explained that he could not stay, for now he was in haste.

The tetrapylon in Aphrodiasias, Asia Minor, gateway to what was the temple of Aphrodite.

CHAPTER 17

Life in Paul's Churches

W hat was church life like in the first century?
What precisely went on in Paul's churches?
The evidence is fragmentary, so exploring it is
like wandering around an unknown church in the dark,
lit by a few flashes of lightning: it is intriguing but
frustratingly random. Paul's letters never offer a blueprint
for church life, but deal with it on the whole only when
troubleshooting is needed, so what we read depends on
what problems happened to arise.

We have several sources of information, rather
different in their usefulness: Paul's definitely genuine
letters; his doubted letters; Acts; uncanonical early
Christian writings; and early non-Christian reports. From
the latter two categories, two writings are especially
informative. The Christian one is the *Didache* or *The
Teaching of the Apostles*, a manual for church life probably
written at the end of the first century, by one of the first
generation or two of church leaders after the death of
the apostles. The non-Christian one is a letter from Pliny,
the governor of Bithyinia in Asia Minor in around AD 112,
reporting to Emperor Trajan on his dealings with
Christians.

All of our informants agree that Christians met for
worship on Sundays. Later writings call it 'the Lord's day',
but Paul and Acts simply call it 'the first day of the week'.
As it was a working day, they must have met before or
after work. There is no record of Christians treating
Sunday as a day of rest until Emperor Constantine
introduced the practice in the fourth century. Acts

mentions an evening meeting in Troas – at which Paul kept going until daybreak, which of course was hardly standard. By the time Pliny wrote fifty-five years later, Christians in Bithynia had long been in the habit of meeting both before and after work, sharing supper in the evening.

Sunday was chosen presumably as the day of Jesus' resurrection, but this does not explain why Christians felt the need to move away from the Jewish sabbath. This probably happened because Paul's generation expected to take part in synagogue worship on the sabbath, and so had to have their own meetings on another day. Thus an arrangement that was supposed to keep Christians united with mainstream Jews ended up as yet another thing separating them into two conflicting religions.

The eucharistic meal. A wall painting from the Saints Peter and Marcellinus catacomb in Rome, third or fourth century.

It is also clear that the churches met in people's houses. Paul mentions those of Priscilla and Aquilla, of Philemon and of a woman called Nympha, for example. We should, in the larger churches such as Corinth at least, probably picture something along the lines of a large house with shop front and workshops, housing slaves and servants, workers and business partners, as well as extended family. Paul could use such a place as a base for work and evangelism as well as worship. We should picture the meeting room as a small hall, rather than a lounge in a private residence with a three-piece suite and a few chairs from the dining room. However, in Troas they met in a poorer, second-floor apartment.

In the meetings, they shared the Lord's supper, sang hymns, prayed and listened to prophecy and teaching. The supper was not a token amount of bread and wine but a full meal, people bringing their own food. Just as the Jewish Passover meal involved someone reciting the story of the exodus, so it seems that in Paul's churches he expected someone to recite the story of Jesus' death as re-enacted in the bread and wine. As mentioned earlier, however, both Acts and the *Didache* make much of the meal without ever connecting it to the death or the body and blood of Jesus. The *Didache*'s liturgy finds quite different symbolism in the bread and wine:

As this broken bread, once dispersed over the hills, was brought together and became one loaf, so may thy Church be brought together from the ends of the earth into thy kingdom.

Some churches, therefore, may have celebrated it as a simple fellowship meal rather than as Holy Communion as we know it. The *Didache* also insists that no unbaptized person should take part.

The churches continued to sing the biblical psalms used in the synagogue, but Christians also quickly composed their own songs of praise to Jesus. Various sayings in Paul's letters are thought probably to be quotations from hymns. The most certain is in Ephesians, though that letter may be post-Pauline:

Sleeper awake!
Rise from the dead,
And Christ will shine on you.

The balance between fixed liturgy led by ministers and extempore prayers, etc., from the congregation is hard to judge precisely from his letters, but much in 1 Corinthians suggests an open, charismatic approach. On the one hand, Paul apparently expects each person to contribute 'a hymn, a lesson, a revelation, a tongue, or an interpretation'. He expects men and women to pray and prophesy. He tells them that a meeting should involve two or three prophecies, each speaker standing down when another has a revelation from God. He is also happy for up to three people to speak publicly in tongues, as long as someone has the gift to interpret them.

On the other hand, many phrases are found in Paul's letters that seem to quote or at least to echo a formal liturgy – which should not surprise us as Jewish worship had plenty. The two that are most definite are the creed that Paul cites in 1 Corinthians 15, though this may have been reserved for baptisms, and the invocation '*Maranatha*' ('Come Lord!'), an Aramaic word that Paul uses in 1 Corinthians 16, and which would have been quite meaningless to Greeks unless they were already familiar with it from their prayers. The *Didache* offers a form of words for Eucharistic prayers, but also says that prophets may use their own words.

'Prophecy' was understood as bringing a message from God. It was not necessarily a prediction of the future, though there are examples of this in Acts. Neither was it necessarily an unpremeditated outburst, though it certainly could be. The term included any proclamation of God's word, and so probably had a large overlap with what we would call 'preaching' today. While Paul was among them, he would doubtless have taken a lot of it upon himself. In his absence, he expected men and women in the church to do it themselves. Not all had the gift, he recognized, but then neither was it the preserve of one church leader alone. He was equally moderate in how he expected Christians to receive prophecy. On the one hand he did not want them to be over-cynical and despise it. On the other hand, he did not want them to accept prophecies uncritically, but weigh up what they said. As he told the Thessalonians, 'Do not despise the words of prophets, but test everything.'

'Teach and admonish one another in all wisdom; and with gratitude in your hearts sing psalms, hymns and spiritual songs to God.'

COLOSSIANS 3:16

An underground chapel from the second or third century in the St Priscilla catacomb in Rome. On the furthest arch is the famous *Fractio Panis*, a fresco depicting men and women breaking bread.

The *Didache* elaborates on this point, saying that hearers are to judge prophets by the soundness of their teaching and conduct (though it has some reservations on the latter, thanks to the less than respectable signs enacted by some scriptural prophets), and by whether they are so unspiritual as to eat while 'in the Spirit'. However, such testing is only to be done in retrospect – to judge a prophet in full flow is the unforgivable blasphemy against the Holy Spirit.

Another major part of worship in Corinth was speaking in tongues. Paul addresses this at length in 1 Corinthians, although he never mentions it in any other letter. Acts also mentions it as a sign of the gift of the Holy Spirit to new believers. It meant speaking in a 'heavenly language', incomprehensible except to those with the God-given power to interpret.

Paul spoke in tongues himself, and apparently considered it a normal part of Christian life – though not a vitally important one, presumably, if he only ever mentions it in the one case where it has got out of control. The problem in Corinth was that it had come to dominate their services, prized as a sign that their communal worship – and those individuals with the gift – were especially full of God's Spirit. Paul's answer to this is that speaking in tongues is invaluable in private prayer and should not be forbidden in public, but it is far more useful for people to hear a message that they can understand. Prophecy and teaching are more valuable for building up the church and should be given priority. He insists that speaking in tongues is one of many different spiritual gifts, and by no means the most important, so the Corinthians should not expect everyone to have it, nor should they over-glamorize it. Its use should be limited to three times at the most in one service, and then only when it can be interpreted. If the message is not made comprehensible, the person is 'speaking into the air'.

Pliny's report on the Christians
Though second-hand and second century, this report from Pliny, the governor of Bithyinia written around AD 112, offers a valuable window into life in early churches such as Paul's:

It was their habit on a fixed day to assemble before daylight and recite by turns a form of words to Christ as a god; and… they bound themselves with an oath, not for any crime, but not to commit theft or robbery or adultery, not to break their

*word, and not to deny a deposit when demanded. After this
was done, their custom was to depart, and to meet again to
take food.*

The most important part of church life beyond weekly
worship was baptism. This was an essential part of
becoming a Christian and joining the church, closely
linked to repentance, faith, the forgiveness of sins and
the gift of the Holy Spirit. The questions of communal and
infant baptism were dealt with earlier. Another way in
which the accounts in Acts stand apart from most later
Christian practice is that converts were baptized instantly
on conversion, even if – as with the Philippian prison
guard – that meant in the middle of the night.

Paul makes no rules for the practice of baptism, but his
talk of being 'buried with [Christ] through baptism' suggests
that believers were lowered into the water. The *Didache*
instructs that Christians should be baptized in a river if
possible; if not, then immersed in water, preferably cold. If
even that is not possible, then sprinkling is also acceptable.
Candidates are to be instructed first about Christian
conduct, and are to fast for a day or two beforehand. Then
they are baptized 'In the name of the Father and of the Son
and of the Holy Ghost'. Acts talks only of baptizing in the
name of Jesus, and Paul makes no rule about whose name
it is done in – as long as it is not his.

Paul and Women

Where Paul has become most unpopular in the modern world is in his attitude to women. He is seen as repressive and negative, a widespread view summed up by a popular British writer and TV personality in a magazine on sale as I write: 'That dreadful, dreadful, Paul! … He hated women.'

This popular judgment is extraordinarily unjust. The harshest informed assessment that can reasonably be made of him is that he repeated what virtually everybody else in his day believed. A fairer appraisal would be that he was one of the most progressive voices in the ancient world.

His condemnation is based on two passages where Paul apparently forbids women to speak in church (1 Corinthians 14:34–35 and 1 Timothy 2:11–15), another where he insists they cover their heads in worship (1 Corinthians 11:3–16), and several where he tells them to submit to their husbands. For example:

As in all the churches of the saints, women should be silent in the churches. For they are not permitted to speak, but should be subordinate, as the Law also says. If there is anything they desire to know, let them ask their husbands at home. For it is shameful for a woman to speak in church.
1 CORINTHIANS 14:34–35

Wives, be subject to your husbands, as is fitting in the Lord. Husbands, love your wives and never treat them harshly.
COLOSSIANS 3:18–19

These certainly sound repressive, but to give Paul a fair hearing we need to make sure that we have understood his meaning right, and placed his instructions where they

> 'People who are afraid to tell God, or even Jesus, how angry they are with him or them, are often glad to be able to take out such anger on someone like Paul.'
>
> N.T. WRIGHT

belong, in the context of first-century Greece and Asia
Minor, not as if they were written in the twenty-first-
century West. We have no space to examine each passage
in depth, so having sketched general attitudes to women
in the ancient world we will look quite closely at what Paul
says about women speaking, followed by brief comments
on the other issues.

Women in the ancient world

In ancient Greece and Rome, women had no political
rights and were expected to be under the rule of father,
husband or, in the case of single adults, a guardian. This
was based on the traditional understanding, as Emperor
Gaius explained, 'that because of their levity of disposition
they are easily deceived'. In classical Athens they had
been expected to stay indoors. They were increasingly
freer in imperial society, but still all that a woman owned –
and in theory her
very life –

Women
harvesting fruit.
A Greek vase
painting from the
fifth century BC.

belonged to her father, even if she married, until he died.

A good woman was universally expected above all to be quiet and submissive. 'Silence is a woman's glory,' said the Greeks. Likewise, 'Her greatest glory is not to be spoken of, whether in praise or blame.' Few people saw any point in teaching women much. Paul's younger contemporary Plutarch was more progressive than most, suggesting that men should educate their wives in philosophy – but precisely because they were so foolish when left to their own ways.

The philosophers had mixed attitudes to women, few of them very wonderful. Souls being sexless, Plato argued controversially that in an ideal world women would be educated just like men and trained for the same roles – even for government. However, one reason for this was precisely that the average woman is less able than the average man at everything and therefore has no special sphere of competence. He had a couple of female disciples, one of whom found it necessary to disguise herself as a man.

His successor Aristotle reasserted the status quo with a vengeance. He saw the sexes as essentially different, man being made for courage and command, woman for obedience and holding her tongue. 'The male is by nature superior, the female inferior; and the one rules, and the other is ruled; this principle, of necessity, extends to all mankind.'

Another younger contemporary of Paul, the Stoic Musonius Rufus, is one of the very few thinkers whose view of women does not now sound shockingly negative. He not only argued that boys and girls should have the same

'A man is best off with a nonentity... Aphrodite inspires more mischief in the clever ones, while a helpless woman is freed from folly by the simplicity of her thoughts.'

EURIPIDES, 428 BC

'I hate the woman... who never breaks the rules and principles of grammar and who quotes verses I never heard of.'

JUVENAL,
FIRST CENTURY

Jesus offends
social
conventions by
talking to a
Samaritan
woman in public.
*Christ and the
Samaritan
Woman at the
Well*, Anibale
Carraci, 1604/5.

education because they have the same mental and moral
abilities, but also advocated something like a reciprocal
relationship between husband and wife, holding their
property in common, caring for each other and looking
out for each other's interests.

Jewish culture was no more positive to women than
pagan culture. Josephus, the first-century historian, wrote,
'The scripture says that a woman is inferior to her
husband in all things. Let her, therefore, be obedient to
him.' Philo, a contemporary philosopher, maintained the
tradition of women staying indoors. The book of *Sirach*,
which would have played a prominent part of Paul's
Pharisaic upbringing, not only reflects pagan ideals for
women ('A silent wife is a gift from the Lord'), but also
says, 'Better is the wickedness of a man than a woman
who does good; it is woman who brings shame and
disgrace.' Men's daily prayers gave thanks for not being
a woman and female testimony was, as elsewhere, not
acceptable in Jewish courts. The great first-century sage

Eliezer ben Hyrcanus said, 'Rather should the words of the Torah be burned than entrusted to a woman... Whoever teaches his daughter the Torah is like one who teaches her obscenity' – though there may in fact have been one or two female synagogue teachers in the Roman world.

The more immediate background to Paul's attitude to women is that of Jesus, of course. We have many examples in the Gospels of Jesus explicitly and implicitly challenging social prejudice and injustice against women, such as his criticism of divorce practice. He also had many female disciples, going so far as to tell Martha, who virtuously stuck to her womanly chores while her sister Mary sat at his feet as a disciple, that Mary had 'chosen the better part'.

However, Jesus said little, as far as we know, to challenge the ideal of quiet submission or the female dress code. None of the twelve was a woman, he appointed none as leaders or teachers, and none of the seventy-two he sent out to proclaim the kingdom of God was said to be a woman.

As for other Christian writings included in the New Testament, none that touches on the role of women has anything less conservative to say than Paul.

Against this background, it should become clear that when 1 Timothy 2:11 says, 'Let a woman learn in silence and full submission', the one thing that might have raised an eyebrow in the Greco-Roman world among Jew or Gentile was not 'in silence and full submission', but 'let a woman learn'.

Women preachers

So even if we take Paul's strictures at face value, he is among the more liberal writers of antiquity and so hardly deserves his special vilification. He expected all Christian women to be disciples as well as worshippers, and to be taught just like men – not merely at second hand by their husbands. The fact that he addresses women with non-Christian husbands shows that he welcomed them independently of their husbands, accepting them into the church on the same basis as men. At the end of Romans, he greets sixteen men and eight women, but he praises four of the eight women for their work, and just two of the sixteen men – quite a lapse for a famous misogynist.

Where he is nothing short of radical is in allowing women to preach in his churches and according them apostolic status. However unwelcome we may find his insistence that Corinthian women cover their heads when prophesying and praying in public, the truly remarkable thing about it is that he assumes without question that women as well as men will regularly proclaim God's word in church.

His letters reveal an impressive list of individual women who held prominent and vocal positions in his churches. We have already met Priscilla, whom he calls his 'fellow-worker'. Similarly he names Euodia and Syntyche in Philippi as women who 'struggled alongside me in the work of the gospel', Mary 'who has worked very hard' in the church in Rome, and also in Rome 'those workers in the Lord, Trypaena and Tryphosa'. Most impressively, he counts a woman called Junia in Rome as a fellow apostle, and one Phoebe as 'a servant of the church at Cenchrae', 'servant' being a term that could mean an administrator (i.e. 'deacon') but usually for Paul means 'minister'.

In this context, Paul's apparent prohibition of women speaking in church makes very little sense, especially in 1 Corinthians, where he has already discussed at some length what women should wear when they prophesy.

One possible solution to this puzzle is that both passages are of doubtful authorship. The case against 1 Timothy (and the other two 'pastoral' letters) being genuinely Paul's is stronger than any other Pauline writings in the Bible. 1 Corinthians is undoubtedly by Paul, but the passage about women speaking may well have found its way in there later. It is found at slightly different points in different manuscripts, and its appeal to the Law sounds unlike Paul.

If it is genuine, then what kind of speaking does Paul have in mind? His instruction that they should address any questions they have to their husbands at home and not be insubordinate in church suggests that he is addressing women who have got into the habit of interrupting the preacher, or maybe of calling comments and questions across the room to their husbands, rather than being concerned with female prophets. It was acceptable in Greco-Roman culture for listeners to interrupt public speakers with intelligent questions, but rude if one's comments betrayed ignorance of the subject – as it surely would for the average uneducated Greek woman. However we interpret the passage, either it does not prohibit women preachers in Corinth, or it is not by Paul.

As for the passage in 1 Timothy, where the writer says, 'I permit no woman to teach or to have authority over a man,' there are various issues, one of which is translation. The language is somewhat obscure, and the statement could well be rendered 'I permit no woman to teach in a way that seizes authority over a man' or 'over her

'Teach and admonish one another in all wisdom; and with gratitude in your hearts sing psalms, hymns and spiritual songs to God.'

COLOSSIANS 3:16

Paul and homosexuality

Paul is central to contemporary debates on whether gay relationships are compatible with Christianity, because apart from two laws in Leviticus, all biblical condemnations of gay sex are in his name.

1 Corinthians 6:9 and 1 Timothy 1:10 condemn *malakoi* and *arsenokoitai*. These terms are hard to translate, the first being vague and the second obscure. They are often taken to describe respectively the 'passive' and 'active' roles between two men. Whether Paul, in that case, had in mind all same-sex activity, or something narrower such as that between client and male prostitute is much debated.

The other passage is Romans 1:24–27. Here Paul says that because pagans worshipped idols, they became degraded, women turning to unnatural intercourse and men to shameless acts with other men. This is traditionally taken as condemning all gay sex, but alternatives are offered. One is that, having been talking about idol-worship, Paul may only have temple prostitution in mind. Another is that Paul is talking about men who abandon their natural attraction to women, and so this only applies to 'experimenting' straight men, not to those who are gay by orientation. A third possibility is that the passage is ironic. Paul is prompting his synagogue-going readers with judgments on the pagan ways that Jews found most offensive, gradually homing in on more universal sins, so that he can spring the trap in Romans 2:1, showing that in condemning these things they have condemned themselves.

Another consideration is that gay sex in the ancient world can be seen as largely exploitative – the shortlived use of adolescents by older men, and of slaves and prostitutes. Paul would have good reason to assume from first-century experience that homosexuality was fundamentally predatory and did not have in his sights the loving marriage of equals.

husband', the emphasis being in each case on violent usurpation rather than simply exercising leadership. If so, the instruction addresses a local problem where particular women are causing difficulties and so it should probably not be understood as a universal ruling about Christian women in general. The evidence of 1 and 2 Timothy as a whole is that the local church was threatened by unorthodox teaching spread by men making canny use of the efficient housewives' circuit.

So even assuming we accept the traditional translation, probably the fairest assessment of this passage is that the writer is not opposing women's teaching in general, but is either taking advantage of, or lapsing into, that universal prejudice in his efforts to contain a local disturbance, unfortunate as that stance may well appear to modern readers.

Moving on to the other questions of women's headdress and wifely submission, the issues in the first are hideously complicated, and we cannot even scratch the surface here. The question for the church involved not just gender roles but sexual morality, class oppression, culture clashes and the matter of rights versus obligations. On top of that we face the linguistic conundrums of what Paul means by man being woman's 'head' (certainly not quite what it sounds in English). The main point, though, must be that in regulating what women wore to preach he was supporting, not opposing, their preaching.

As for wives submitting to husbands, the instructions are all from letters of questioned authorship, but Colossians (quoted above) is the one most likely to be genuinely Paul's. Many ancient teachers instructed readers how to govern their wives, children and slaves. Wives were generally uneducated, closeted, inexperienced and half the age of their husbands, so for many men they had little to offer but legitimate procreation and they were universally expected to be subject to their husbands in every way. In such a context, for Paul, like everyone else, to expect a wife to submit was not a great moral failing.

What is far more remarkable is that his demands are reciprocal, stressing a man's obligations towards his wife (and children) just as much as theirs towards him.

One more important point is that Roman society was deeply suspicious of Eastern religious cults, especially of their threat to family values, a suspicion sometimes expressed in violent suppression. Paul's gospel was in many ways thoroughly subversive, but that meant he had to choose his battleground, and we cannot blame him if he did not want the issue over which he took on the Roman empire to be woman's clothing or her right to answer her husband back.

A fair assessment of Paul's attitude to women must accept that he was an influence for liberation and dignity. If instructions he wrote to churches in the Roman empire sound repressive when transplanted into the modern West, it is because we are 2,000 years further down a path that he had been forging for twenty. Those who are truest to his values today are not those who try to turn the clock back, but those who continue in the direction that he led in.

'You Foolish Galatians!'

When Paul left Corinth around AD 51 after his eighteen-month stay, suddenly he was in a hurry. He returned home so hastily that even when invited to stay in Ephesus – a goal of his mission for a number of years now – all he could offer them was a promise to come back as soon as possible.

Acts gives us no indication of what the urgency was, merely saying that once back in Palestine Paul paid a quick visit either to the church in Caesarea or Jerusalem (it is not clear which) and a longer one to Antioch, and then took a tour once again around the churches of Galatia.

Judging from Paul's letters, though, it seems that the circumcision dispute had broken out again, and more dangerously than ever. Not all Christians were satisfied with the result of the Jerusalem council, and some Jerusalem Christians remained convinced that failing to circumcise Gentile converts into the law of Moses was a deluded betrayal of the gospel of Jesus. Taking a leaf out of Paul's book, they had been taking their own missionary journeys to win Gentiles to full Mosaic Christianity, including Paul's own churches. Whether they tried their luck in Antioch again, we have no idea, but they went round Galatia and later followed his trail into Macedonia.

This presumably is when Paul wrote his furious letter to the Galatians. As we have seen, this timing is only half certain, because the letter and the campaign that occasioned it may equally have come before the Jerusalem council. Either way, though, Paul's polemic in later letters shows that the conflict continued passionately, so we will

not be going far wrong if we place the Galatian troubles
here.

Admittedly Acts claims no knowledge of this, but it fits
well with what it does (and does not) tell us. For one thing,
it explains Paul's mysterious hurry to return east from
Corinth. For another, Acts knows nothing about any of
Paul's letter-writing so it may as well slot in here as
elsewhere. And for a third, Acts makes no mention of the
circumcision dispute continuing beyond the Jerusalem
council, despite the fact that Paul's letters show that it did.

Such silence from Acts is understandable. Both for
aesthetic and polemical reasons, one can see why Luke
would not be inclined to describe the dragging out of a
theological dispute that as far as he was concerned was
resolved decisively at the council. So if we know from Acts
that Paul had urgent but unspecified business to attend
to, and we know from the letters that the circumcision
conflict continued to be a major concern for him, then it
makes good sense to put the two together.

In addition to the theological arguments that they
had used in Antioch, the circumcisers explicitly tried to
undermine Paul's authority. They themselves, they told
the Galatians, were members of the mother church, the
church of the apostles. They had been appointed to office

by the apostles, and the full Jewish gospel by which they lived was the same as theirs. Paul, in contrast, was a renegade and a maverick. His watered-down teaching did not have the authority of Jerusalem, and he had disagreed about it with Peter and even Barnabas.

This is why a main theme of Galatians, second only to the pointlessness of Gentile circumcision, is Paul's defence of his own authority. It bursts in with the first word of the letter after his name. Translated literally: 'Paul, apostle, not from men, nor by men, but through Jesus Christ and God [the] Father'.

He argues first that the authority of Jerusalem is meaningless. The circumcisers claim to be speaking on behalf of the Jerusalem apostles, but those apostles are only human and Paul has his message from God. It is in this context that he makes the intriguing, and one would think exaggerated, claim that he learned nothing about the gospel from the apostles or any other Christians, but received it all directly from God. When this happened, he conferred with nobody. When he finally met up with the Jerusalem leaders fifteen years later, they added nothing to it.

If anything, Paul suggests his authority is equal to that of the apostles themselves, the only difference being their audience: Peter sent to the Jews; Paul to the Gentiles. However, he evidently does not want to get into comparative authorities: he is a true apostle with the true gospel from God; whatever anyone else is or has is beside the point.

Paul has a tightrope to walk here. Any suggestion that his gospel is in conflict with Jerusalem would play into the circumcisers' dangerous hands. Yet any suggestion that Jerusalem have approved his gospel would equally undermine his independent authority. So on the one hand he assures readers that he has made his teaching clear to the alleged pillars of Jerusalem, and that they saw no reason to add to it, but recognized the grace God had given him and praised God because of him. On the other hand he insists that he couldn't care less what authority other Christians invest in these people. They are called pillars,

Paul's travels,
AD 51–52.

0   200 miles

0   200 km

but 'what they actually were makes no difference to me; God shows no partiality'. If they (or Paul himself or an angel from heaven) had contradicted the gospel God had revealed to Paul, they would have been wrong.

Paul wrote this impassioned philippic at some point between hearing the bad news in Corinth and his return to Galatia. The only indication we have of how successful he was in winning the Galatians back is the fact that the letter survives, suggesting that it was revered by at least some of the churches in the region, and that he was able to collect money from them for his later gift to Jerusalem.

His unhappy business in Galatia complete, Paul took the west road back to Ephesus. We are now on what is called Paul's third missionary journey, although that numbering is somewhat misleading. It implies that in coming to Jerusalem or Antioch Paul was returning home on leave before setting out again on new travels. In fact, his visit to Antioch was a brief, businesslike call as part of his preaching tour against the circumcisers. After AD 48, when he fell out with Peter and Barnabas and left Antioch with Silas, he seems to have called nowhere home, travelling continuously, his only sedentary times being his long stays in Corinth and Ephesus, and his later captivity.

Ephesus at Last

Paul stayed in Ephesus for three years, from AD 52 to 55. Acts has disappointingly little information about Paul's escapades here considering the length and success of his visit, and Paul's letters add little.

He fulfilled his invitation to expound his teaching in the synagogue, and managed to keep it up for a record three months before outstaying their good will. From then on he taught and debated daily in a lecture hall. According to an ancient alternative version of Acts, the 'western text', Paul occupied it from 11 a.m. until 4 p.m., perhaps when the school was closed for siesta. In the morning and afternoon, he worked.

There were already Christians in Ephesus before Paul arrived, including Priscilla and Aquilla whom Paul had left there on his flying visit earlier in the year, and believers met in their house. Another was a keen but under-instructed preacher called Apollos. He was an Alexandrian Jew and a follower of John the Baptist, whose movement was still going strong after his death. Apollos also believed that Jesus was the messiah and had added this to his preaching, though he did not know the full gospel as Paul would recognize it. He came to Ephesus between Paul's two visits. He preached successfully, but Priscilla and Aquilla had to take him to one side and give him fuller Christian instruction.

By the time Paul came, Apollos had moved on to Corinth – where their paths would cross again – and it seems Paul felt he had some mopping up to do. He found a group of about twelve converts – presumably Apollos's – who believed in Jesus but had never heard of the Holy Spirit. The Spirit was vital to Paul's Christianity, living in individual believers, inspiring evangelism, prophecy and

'You are initiated into the mysteries of the gospel with Paul, the holy, the martyred, the deservedly most happy, at whose feet may I be found, when I reach God, who mentions you in Christ Jesus in all his letters.'

IGNATIUS, C. 100, TO EPHESUS

worship, working miracles and making them holy. So he probed further and found that Apollos had not baptized them in the name of Jesus, but only with the baptism of repentance that he had learned from John. For Paul, the gift of the Spirit was tied to Christian baptism, so he rebaptized them in the name of Jesus, and Acts says that the Holy Spirit came upon them and they spoke in tongues and prophesied.

Being a centre for magic, it is appropriate that Ephesus was the setting for Paul's greatest display of the miraculous power of Jesus. According to Acts, 'God was performing extraordinary miracles by the hands of Paul, so that handkerchiefs or aprons were even carried from his body to the sick, and the diseases left them and the evil spirits went out.' Such claims are naturally taken as the 'stamp of legend' on Acts' account by many scholars, but we have already seen that those who discount healings

Ephesus

Ephesus, on the Aegean coast of Asia Minor, was one of the most important and richest cities in the empire. In Paul's eyes it must also have seemed one of the spiritually darkest. It was a centre for emperor worship and magic, and among many other cults the city was devoted above all to the goddess Artemis. Her temple there was the largest building in the world, one of the seven wonders, and boasted 127 pillars. One survives. In later years it hosted two of the church's many councils to debate its teachings about Christ.

and such acts of power have not only Luke but also Paul
to reckon with, who was convinced that his ministry was
approved by miracles, and it is natural that Ephesus
should see its share. Christians were not sceptical about
magic (very few people were), so Paul's job was not to
disprove its claims but to prove that it was evil and that
Jesus' power was greater. It was a contest not unlike
Elijah's with the prophets of Baal, though in this case
the losers were not executed.

Paul's display was compelling enough for many
Ephesians to join the church. Converts publicly burned
their scrolls – someone calculated the total came to a
value of 50,000 denarii, a year's wages for 200 people. Paul
was impressive enough to earn not only converts but also
imitators, and a number of Jewish exorcists started to cast
out spirits in the name of Jesus. Acts mentions the seven
sons of an alleged Jewish high priest, who got into trouble

The one
remaining pillar
of the temple
of Artemis
at Ephesus.

trying this. Crying, 'Jesus I know, and Paul I know, but who are you?', the demoniac overpowered the seven of them till they fled naked and wounded, Acts says. Such a story could, of course, only magnify Paul's impact on Ephesus.

Once he was settled in Ephesus, Paul used it as a base for mission to the rest of the province of Asia. Sometimes he went himself to nearby cities; sometimes he sent

others, such as Epaphras who went in his name to Colossae, Laodicea and Hierapolis. At some point he even went up into Illyricum, the region that we know as Slavic.

From this picture that Acts gives us of Paul in Ephesus, it should have been the high point of his apostolic career. But this is probably little more than a few snapshots from his early months there, and from his letters a rather darker picture emerges. He gave a mixed report to the Corinthians – 'a wide door for effective work has opened to me, and there are many adversaries'. In the same letter he says, 'I fought with wild beasts in Ephesus', which could conceivably be meant literally but is probably a figure of speech, and 'I die every day' which certainly is. What he said on leaving Ephesus is more extreme still:

We do not want you to be unaware, brothers and sisters, of the affliction we experienced in Asia; for we were so utterly, unbearably crushed that we despaired of life itself. Indeed, we felt that we had received the sentence of death so that we would rely not on ourselves but on God who raises the dead.
2 CORINTHIANS 1:8–9

His comment that Priscilla and Aquilla 'risked their necks for my life' probably refers to Ephesus too.

We have little idea what specific troubles so plagued Paul here. His 'hardship lists', written shortly afterwards, mention imprisonments, floggings, beatings, and three shipwrecks, one of which left him adrift at sea for twenty-four hours. The most common conclusion is that Paul spent some time in prison in Ephesus.

Bad news from Corinth

It is more likely than not that Paul made trips to other churches while he was based at Ephesus, or at least sent representatives such as Timothy, Titus and Epaphras.

The case we know most about is Corinth. Paul sent a messenger there with a general letter of encouragement, reminding them of his teaching and exhorting them to

Opposite page:
The Ephesians burn their magic books. *The Sermon of St Paul at Ephesus,* by Eustache Le Sueur, 1649.

'Owing to envy, Paul also obtained the reward of patient endurance, after being seven times thrown into captivity, compelled to flee, and stoned.'
CLEMENT OF ROME, C. 96

keep going in the Christian life. The Corinthians were remiss enough not to preserve it.

Later, Paul received several visitors from Corinth, with news and enquiries. The picture of the church that Paul got from these visitors was quite alarming – disputes, divisions and deviation on the most basic moral and theological matters.

The greatest division was caused by a visit from Apollos, who had come to Corinth shortly after Paul had left. Like Paul, he preached successfully, and the church grew. In fact, his preaching may well have been rather more successful than Paul's; certainly many listeners found it more impressive. He was a well-trained orator, and coming from Alexandria he may have learned Philo's technique of using allegorical interpretation to uncover the hidden wisdom of the Jewish scriptures. Luke says that he was 'an eloquent man, and mighty in the scriptures', whereas Paul says of himself in this context that he was sent to proclaim the gospel 'not with eloquent wisdom, so that the cross of Christ might not be emptied of its power'. After Apollos left, the church split into factions, one proclaiming allegiance to Paul and another to Apollos.

To compound the problem, Peter or his assistants had dropped by on their own missionary travels, and this created a third faction, in his name. Others wanted nothing to do with any leadership cult and so dissociated themselves from the three groups, saying they followed none but Christ. So now there was a fourth faction. They were so divided that members were known to take each other to court.

There were other quite different divisions in Corinth too. There were class divisions, manifest most seriously at communion, where wealthy hosts and their friends feasted, while many of the working majority went without through working late. And lastly there were divisions between ordinary Christians and those who were considered, at least by themselves, to be filled with the Holy Spirit – probably quite a large proportion of the church. They spoke publicly in tongues, which was taken as evidence of their spiritual status.

Some scholars link the other main problems at Corinth that Paul now heard about to this Spirit-filled élite. This is quite plausible, though Paul does not explicitly connect them himself so it is not certain. One was sexual licence: a man was sleeping with his father's wife and others used prostitutes. Many of the church were quite happy with this – their freedom from traditional moral codes was evidence that they lived by the Spirit and followed his will alone. 'All things are lawful for me,' was their slogan, picking up on Paul's teaching that the law of Moses no longer applies to those who have the Spirit. Then at the other extreme, some were teaching that Christians should be celibate.

1 Corinthians

Paul's response was to write to Corinth again, the letter we know as 1 Corinthians, dealing one by one with each of these problems. First, and at greatest length, Paul dealt with the faction crisis. He utterly condemned all divisions and appealed for unity, while at the same time defending his ministry from those who disparaged it for lacking the eloquence and wisdom of Apollos's.

This can be read in very different ways. On the one hand, Paul the selfless servant of Christ refuses to support one side or the other, even the Paul faction, and declines to enter the debate, to the extent that we have no idea what issues actually divided them. He has to answer charges against his preaching where they reflect badly on his gospel, but at the same time by contrasting the 'foolishness' of God with human 'wisdom' he is aiming to cure them of all hero worship.

On the other hand, you could argue that it was entirely in Paul's interest to end the leadership cults as Apollos had the larger following; and that under the cover of a call for unity he makes an extensive assault on Apollos's standing. In scorning eloquence, 'lofty words',

'Read your letter from the blessed Apostle Paul again... Even at that time you had been setting up favourites of your own.'

CLEMENT OF ROME, C. 96, TO CORINTH

'the wisdom of the world' and 'the debater of this age' he undermines all the things that recommended Apollos. He says that both of them are merely 'servants through whom you came to believe', but when he adds that 'I planted, Apollos watered, but God gave the growth', and that 'like a skilled master builder I laid a foundation, and someone else is building on it', the implication seems to be that much of the credit for Apollos's success should go to Paul.

Doubtless the truth has something of both interpretations, although we cannot know how much without knowing more of the background. It was for the sake of the church and Christ and for his own sake that Paul wanted unity, and though he clearly meant to reclaim some of his former kudos at Corinth at the expense of Apollos, the fact that at the same time he was urging Apollos to visit them suggests that he honestly saw him as a fellow-worker and not just as a rival.

Other matters were more straightforward. Paul utterly condemned the man who slept with his father's wife, telling the church to expel him, and the use of prostitutes, which for those who are part of Christ's body, he said, was like forcing Christ into a liaison with a prostitute. He condemned lawsuits between Christians too: they would judge all the world at the coming of Christ, so what were they doing asking pagans to judge them?

His attitude to those who taught celibacy was more nuanced. There was nothing at all wrong with marriage and the relationship should be sexual. Divorce was wholly unacceptable. However, he had great sympathy for those who chose to stay single to serve the Lord with undivided attention. This was his own path and it was the better way. Moreover, the imminent return of the Lord and the turbulent events expected to precede it made Christian mission too urgent and dangerous for divided loyalties, so in view of this Paul called on all who could manage it to stay unmarried. And yet he recognized that not everyone was built for celibacy, conceding that those who doubted their willpower were free to marry.

Coming to the questions of worship, he insisted that at communion all should eat together, putting aside any divisions, and waiting for those who work late. As for speaking in tongues, Paul says it is a good thing which he does more than anyone, though it is more for private prayer than public worship. But where the Corinthians have really gone wrong is making it *the* gift of the Spirit, the badge of a Spirit-filled life. Paul urgently downplays its importance – it is one of many gifts of the Spirit and by no means the most important, having limited value in building up the church. Prophecy in particular is far more worthy of their obsession, but loving people is more important than all. Hence it is in the middle of this really rather obscure discussion about the use and value of speaking in tongues that Paul wrote his most celebrated passage of all on the importance of love.

The climax of the letter is Paul's reaffirmation of the bodily resurrection of the dead. He insists it is a literal future rising, not a metaphorical, spiritual rebirth – although the resurrected flesh will be very different and more 'spiritual'. He argues that the resurrection of Christ, the cornerstone of the faith, would be impossible if one denies resurrection. It is integrally tied up with the resurrection of all believers, being the first fruits of the harvest of those who have become one with him. If there is no resurrection for those like Paul who have embraced a life of trouble for the gospel, then it is futile and 'we are of all people most to be pitied'.

Timothy took this letter to Corinth around AD 55. It has been read with such devotion by Christians over the centuries that it is easy to assume that its rebukes, encouragement and teachings knocked the church right back on the rails. In fact, Paul's troubled vexations over Corinth were to get much worse before they got better.

'If I have the gift of prophecy and can fathom all mysteries and all knowledge, and if I have a faith that can move mountains, but have not love, I am nothing.'

1 CORINTHIANS 13:2

CHAPTER 21

The Jerusalem Lynch Mob

aul made a dramatic exit from Ephesus. He had
already planned to go to Jerusalem via Macedonia
and Greece, but a riot rather forced his hand.

It started with Artemis, who was the centre not only of
the Ephesians' worship but also of their economy. Enough
people had become Christians in three years for artisans –
for example, the silversmith Demetrius, who made shrines –
to feel threatened. He rounded up
others for a public protest, with
the slogan 'Great is Artemis of
the Ephesians.' This tapped in to
Ephesian paranoia about Paul's
alien cult subverting their
traditions, and soon a riot had
started. They found two foreign
missionaries, the Corinthians
Gaius and Aristarchus, and
dragged them into the arena.
Paul was reluctantly persuaded
not to show his face, and after a
couple of hours the town clerk
managed to restore order, without
the two men being injured.

This was Paul's cue to move
on, and he set off on his tour of
Macedonia and Greece, also
sending representatives to
Galatia. The idea of a collection
for the impoverished Jerusalem

church had been on his mind for a while, and he had asked his churches to save towards it, telling each one how eager the others were to contribute. What had reduced Jerusalem to this poverty we do not know – perhaps famine, anti-Christian policies or their earlier experiments in communism.

Paul's motives are debated. He naturally talked about it in terms of sheer charity, and the Gentiles' chance to do something in return for the gift of the gospel, but it was probably something of a peace offering as well. Paul's Law-free gospel was still terribly controversial in Palestine and the size of the offering would demonstrate its God-given success. In accepting the money, Paul hoped, Jerusalem would be accepting the uncircumcised as brothers and Paul's gospel as one with theirs.

However, the collection was not completed for another

**The theatre at
Ephesus.**

Paul's offering
tour, AD 55–57.

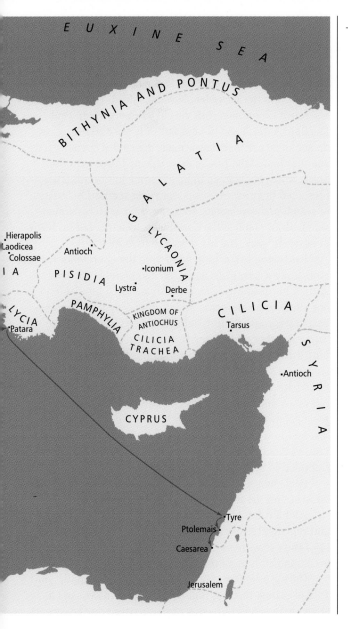

year or two owing to new problems at Corinth, which showed
how imperative friendship with Jerusalem was. Jewish
Christians came to Corinth calling themselves apostles and
exhorted the Corinthians to follow Jewish traditions and
laws. They vigorously attacked Paul and invited Corinth to
align itself to the Jerusalem leaders instead. They obviously
had much in common with the circumcisers whom Paul
fought in Antioch and Galatia, but with two differences: we
do not know whether they actually demanded circumcision;
and they linked the Law to experiencing the power of the
Spirit, which guaranteed them a hearing in Corinth. They
presented themselves as superior Hebrew apostles, boasting
of visions and revelations. Paul, they said, lived by human
standards. He bullied the Corinthians by letter 'but his bodily
presence is weak, and his speech contemptible'.

Paul came to Corinth, and found the church not just
embracing wrong ideas again but completely rebelling
against his authority. One member insulted him, and no
one came to his defence. He left humiliated, and wrote a
desperate, caustic letter, defending himself against the
'superapostles' and calling the Corinthians to return to
him. Titus took the letter without any great hope of
success, it seems, but in fact they repented and were again
filled with zeal for Paul. He then wrote a fourth letter,
full of joy and consolation, celebrating the ministry of
reconciliation, asking them to forgive the man who had
insulted him and again appealing to them to stay true to
him. Parts of these two letters, and perhaps others, were
compiled to make 2 Corinthians.

Paul spent the winter in Corinth, and it was there that
he wrote his great letter to the Christians in Rome.

Paul left for Jerusalem in AD 57 bringing both money
and representatives from his churches. The writer of Acts
or of the eye-witness passages at least, if they are genuine,
accompanied him all the way.

During a week's stay in Troas on the Asia Minor coast,
Paul preached through Sunday night until dawn, and a
young man called Eutychus who was sitting in the second-

floor window fell asleep and fell to the ground. Paul went down, took him in his arms, said, 'Do not be alarmed, for his life is in him,' and then went back to his sermon. The narrator tells us he had raised the dead.

Paul then summoned the Ephesian church leaders and bid them an emotional farewell. His evangelistic work was done in this area and it was time to look west into Europe.

Landing in Palestine, they stayed a week with Philip,

Paul's letter to Rome

Romans is Paul's *magnum opus*. Unlike his other letters, it addresses several communities – Gentile Christians, Jewish Christians and Jewish non-Christians – that he has never met. This was his chance to lay out his gospel, address the continuing problem of Gentiles and the Law, and help Jews and Gentiles to live in unity.

He starts cunningly, aiming to trap Jewish hearers into conceding that they do not truly keep the law of Moses and so circumcision does not make them right with God. There are great blessings in being Jewish (Gentiles take note), but all sin against the Law and so cannot be reconciled to God through the Law. How then? Just as all humanity was divorced from God through Adam's sin, so we are reconciled to God through the obedience of Jesus. What happens is that when we are baptized into Christ we become part of his death and resurrection, our old sinful self crucified with him, and new holy life raised within us. (Thus the accusation that his teaching of grace not works invites followers to sin is nonsense.) The Law was not bad, but it only ruled one's mind, while sin ruled one's body. Christ, by coming bodily, conquered sin in the human body, bringing a new spiritual law with glorious rewards.

Paul agonizes over fellow Jews' rejection of the gospel. However, God has a right to choose and reject whom he will – though in fact he has not rejected them. He has kept a remnant, and only hardened the others' hearts temporarily, for the sake of harvesting the Gentiles. When their number is complete, Israel will be reaped.

Paul finishes with a summons to Jewish and Gentile Christians to live holy lives, united in Christ and in love. Some will follow the Law and some not, but let neither side judge, dishonour or offend the other.

*'No man verily
can read it too
oft, or study it
too well; for the
more it is
studied, the
easier it is; the
more it is
chewed, the
pleasanter it is;
and the more
groundly it is
searched, the
preciouser
things are found
in it.'*

WILLIAM TYNDALE,
SIXTEENTH CENTURY,
ON ROMANS

one of the seven, in Caesarea. Both in Tyre and Caesarea prophets warned Paul not to go to Jerusalem because of the danger, and his travelling companions agreed. For non-Christians there, Paul was a blasphemous apostate, preaching against the law of Moses. Even the Jerusalem Christians viewed him with mixed feelings – as a zealous evangelist, but an overly radical one who made life very difficult for them. Paul was unswayable, but he must have gone in some trepidation, for there was no knowing how his offering would be received. He had felt the need to ask the Roman church to pray 'that I may be rescued from the unbelievers in Judea, and that my ministry to Jerusalem may be acceptable to the saints'.

It is hard to say how the offering was in fact received. Paul's later letters never mention it, and amazingly, neither does Acts' account of the visit, though it is detailed and in the first person. If the writer has no knowledge of the offering, it surely means that the 'we' passages were not by a genuine eyewitness (or even a well-informed chronicler). If, alternatively, he deliberately chose not to mention the money, that suggests it was embarrassingly ill received by the church. Then again, Acts later has Paul say that he 'came to bring alms to my nation', which suggests that Luke knew of the offering but did not share Paul's understanding of its significance.

Paul's meeting with James reads cordially in Acts. Paul tells him and the elders about his successes among the Gentiles, and they are delighted. James says that false reports are circulating that Paul is encouraging Jews to abandon the law of Moses, so to reassure Jewish Christians he should join four others who are undergoing a seven-day purification ritual involving sacrifices and head-shaving, and pay the costs for the five of them. He also tells Paul that he has sent instructions to the Gentile churches – the same instructions Acts already quoted as his decree at the Jerusalem council.

The meeting seems a little less genial when viewed against the background of Paul's letters. He and fellow

Jewish missionaries had indeed lived without the Law, so James seems to be asking him, if not to betray, at least to compromise that radicalism in a public display of orthodoxy. The idea that he needed purification on returning from the Gentiles hardly sits well with Paul's own beliefs. And James's letter to the Gentiles might be seen both as a claim of authority and a summons to orthodoxy for the Jews in Paul's churches. Possibly Paul's acquiescence to all this was James's condition for accepting his offering.

Paul was in an invidious position. He was happy to live by the Law when among Jews, but could he obey James without being compromised? Then again maybe compromise was what was needed to make peace with Jerusalem – why let all his labours come to nothing for the sake of a harmless ritual?

In the end, Paul agreed, but he never completed the rite. Before the week was up, he was seen by an opponent who recognized him from Ephesus and raised the alarm. Once again Paul was the centre of a huge riot, and this time his life was saved by Roman troops who intervened and arrested him to restore order. Bound in chains, he persuaded the tribune to let him address the crowd. He told them his story, how he had zealously persecuted Christians until he met Jesus on the road to Damascus, but when he came to his mission to the Gentiles the uproar started again.

The tribune took him to be interrogated with the help of a leather-and-knucklebone whip to establish what his crime had been, which is when Paul announced his Roman citizenship. Since this gave him immunity from flogging, the tribune ordered the Jewish council to question him instead. Here Paul tried to divide the Pharisees against the Sadducees, saying that he was a Pharisee himself, here because of his belief in the resurrection. This won over some Pharisees, but again provoked such violent dissension that the soldiers had to take him away to the barracks. That night, Acts says, Jesus came to him and said, 'Keep up your courage! For just as you have testified for me in Jerusalem, so you must bear witness also in Rome.'

Paul was transferred under armed guard to Caesarea, a less volatile city and the seat of the governor Felix, after a plot emerged to ambush and kill Paul between the barracks and the council. Forty men had made an unfortunate vow to eat nothing until he was dead, but Paul's nephew informed on them.

Felix heard serious accusations of sedition against Paul from the Jewish authorities, but Paul replied that his only offence was a doctrinal one, which would not concern

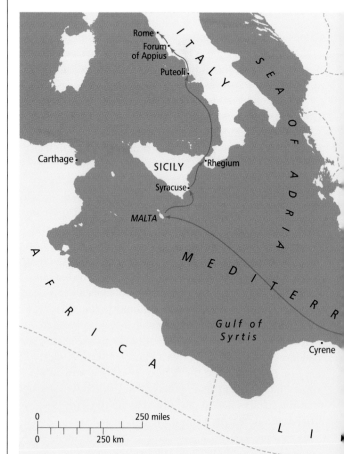

Paul's journey to Rome.

Rome. Felix adjourned the trial on the pretext of wanting an objective report from the tribune, but in fact kept Paul in chains for two years, which diffused an explosive situation, though doubtless dismaying forty hungry Jews. He repeatedly interviewed Paul about Christianity, Acts says, hoping to be offered a bribe. It may well have been now that Paul wrote some of his 'captivity letters'.

It was a change of governor in about AD 59 that set the ball rolling again. When Festus took charge of Judea, the

Shipwrecked on
Malta, Paul is
clasped by a
snake, but not
hurt. *Paul
Arrested on the
Journey to Rome*,
by Matthaeus
Merian the Elder,
1630.

Jewish council appealed for Paul to be sent to them for trial. This would surely have been fatal, and so Paul played his last trump card: he claimed his right as a citizen to be tried at Caesar's court in Rome. Paul had long intended to visit Rome, though not in chains and only briefly as his main goal now was Spain, Rome requiring less evangelism as it already had a thriving church. He was to stay longer than he had intended.

The journey to Rome is a vividly detailed, dramatic story in Acts. Still accompanied by some of the friends from his churches, apparently including the narrator, Paul was taken with other prisoners by sea. They made such slow progress along the coast of Asia Minor that, with

autumn coming on, Paul warned the centurion that lives would be lost if they did not winter in Asia. Unlike other prophecies in Acts, this was not fulfilled. The captain and shipowner wanted to push on to Crete, so unsurprisingly the centurion overruled his prisoner. But as they came round the underside of Crete a violent wind seized them, and they were driven for days, flinging cargo and tackle into the sea to save the ship, seeing neither sun nor moon.

After two weeks adrift, they ran aground off Malta, and the ship broke up. By swimming or holding on to bits of ship, they all reached land safely. As they and the natives gathered wood for a fire, Paul was putting a bundle of brushwood onto the fire when a snake came out of it

and fastened to his hand. Having survived a wreck only to be killed by a beast, the natives thought he must be a murderer, but when he shook it off unharmed they decided he was a god. Doubtless Paul repudiated the idea, but not very effectively: they took him to their leader Publius, whose father had dysentery, and he healed him.

They stayed three months on Malta, and in the spring left on a ship that took them to Puteoli on the west coast of Italy, from where they travelled 100 miles over land. 'And so,' says Luke, 'we came to Rome.'

A statue of Paul at St Paul's Bay, Malta.

CHAPTER 22

Rome and Beyond

The close of Paul's life is just as veiled in mystery as any part of it, which is saying something. Acts depicts him living in Rome for two years under a pretty relaxed house arrest, 'proclaiming the kingdom of God and teaching about the Lord Jesus Christ with all boldness and without hindrance'. And there Acts suddenly and unaccountably stops, leaving two large questions hanging in the air: why, and what happened next?

But before we consider them, there is the issue of what Paul did in the meantime, because he is traditionally held to have written his seven 'captivity letters' in Rome: Philippians; Philemon; Colossians; Ephesians; and the 'pastoral letters' – 1 and 2 Timothy and Titus. Only the first two are unquestionably by Paul, and, while all but 1 Timothy and Titus mention his imprisonment, only 2 Timothy mentions Rome; so the others, even if genuine, could be from earlier imprisonments. Hence they tell us nothing certain about Paul's time in Rome.

They do give us some suggestions, though. The

A view of Rome
showing the
forum.

pastoral letters are more preoccupied than other letters with good order in the church and the roles of different leaders. One can see how, separated from his churches, perhaps forever, building a permanent structure might become important to him.

Philippians, Colossians and Ephesians present us with a more divine, cosmic Christ than Paul's other letters. In Philippians, Jesus is not just a human exalted to heaven, but rather came down from heaven to be born human in the first place. In Colossians (which is much more likely than not to be genuinely Paul's), Christ plays an integral part in the creation of the universe, is the image and embodiment of God, and will reconcile the whole cosmos to him. Colossians and Ephesians both explore the mystic union between Christ and the church further than earlier letters. Perhaps a more exalted sense of who Jesus was grew in Paul during these last years.

Philippians also contains Paul's most violent denunciation of the circumcisers – 'the dogs... those who mutilate the flesh' – so if that came from Rome, the fight continued fiercely.

So, then, why does Acts stop here? The obvious and traditional answer is that Luke wrote it while he was in Rome with Paul and this brings him up to date. For many scholars, however, Acts betrays such distance from the Paul we know from his letters that this is impossible. Unfortunately, every other explanation as to why he would choose to stop here is equally incredible. Acts has carefully followed the progress of Paul's trial for eight chapters. Could Luke conceivably think the result not worth mentioning, even hinting at? If Paul was executed in Rome it is unthinkable that Luke would fail to crown Paul's life with a glorious, Christlike martyrdom. If he was released, then his vindication in the heart of the empire would also suit Luke's apologetic admirably.

One scholar has suggested that neither happened: Paul was left to rot, abandoned by the church, and this humiliation explains Luke's silence. It is an ingenious solution, but pure conjecture defying almost all the evidence of what actually happened to him. Others suggest that he intended to write another sequel, but there is no evidence for this and two years before the end of Paul's life would seem a peculiar place to make the break.

The puzzle is insoluble, and it is perfectly in character that this is what Acts leaves us with.

What then happened to Paul in Rome? Tradition has it that he was released and went to Spain. The earliest information we have is Clement's letter to Corinth, written in about AD 96, reminding the Corinthians of how Paul reached the 'furthest limits of the west' before he died. As Clement was writing in Rome, this must refer to Spain, the only question being whether Clement has it on good authority, or simply deduced it from Paul's saying in Romans that he planned to go there from Rome.

The *Acts of Peter*, written 100 years or so after Paul's death, agrees that Paul went to Spain, although it is a somewhat unreliable book, featuring such delights as a talking dog and a resurrected kipper.

Around the same time, the Muratorian canon, an explanation of which books the church of Rome accepted as canonical, notes with some surprise that Acts omits Paul's visit to Spain and Peter's martyrdom. Some argue that the Romans only knew these stories from the *Acts of Peter*, but as that was a recent writing which they considered spurious, it is more likely that they knew older stories about Paul which the *Acts of Peter* also incorporated.

Thus it seems more likely than not that Paul did indeed get to Spain, having been released from prison after two years in AD 62. If so, however, he does not seem to have been there for long, because tradition places him back in Rome during Nero's massacre of the Christians three years later.

We know a fair bit about this massacre from Roman historians – it is the first time Christians made a

significant impact on pagan history. It started with the fire that devastated Rome in AD 64. Rumour said that Nero started it so that he could rebuild the city, and said it persistently enough that he was driven to find a scapegoat, choosing the few people in Rome less popular than he. He rounded them up and killed them in vast numbers. To add to the entertainment, they were thrown to the dogs dressed in animal skins, crucified or burned as

Nero burns Christians as torches. *The Torches of Nero*, Henryk Siemiradzki, 1876.

*'After preaching
both in the east
and west, he
gained the
illustrious
reputation due
to his faith,
having taught
righteousness to
the whole world,
and come to the
extreme limit of
the west, and
suffered
martyrdom
under the
prefects.'*

CLEMENT OF ROME,
C. 96

living torches to light Nero's garden parties.

According to tradition, Peter and Paul were both killed in this onslaught, though the evidence for this is on the slim side. Clement says only that Paul 'suffered martyrdom under the prefects', and even that could be translated simply 'bore witness before rulers'. One hundred years after Paul's death, the Bishop of Corinth mentioned in a letter to Rome that Peter and Paul had been martyred there at the same time. By about AD 200 a Christian apologist could point to Paul's monument on the Ostian way three miles outside the city and Peter's on Vatican Hill, as evidence that the apostles died there, which demonstrates a long-established tradition. (They are now marked by the great churches of St Peter's and St Paul's Outside the Wall.) Also around AD 200, the great writer Tertullian says that Paul was beheaded in Rome and Peter crucified – the difference being because citizens were not crucified.

So we have quite good evidence that Peter and Paul were executed in Rome, but it is only the *Acts of Paul*, late in the second century, that connects their death with Nero's genocide. This *Acts* is in much the same vein as the fantastical *Acts of Peter*, recounting that when Paul's head was cut off milk spurted out. It is easy to see how the storyteller, knowing that Paul died in Rome in the time of Nero, might make the connection between this and the massacre for himself.

It seems likely then that Paul was beheaded a few miles outside the city of Rome in the mid-sixties, and we know no more of the circumstances of his death than that. What we do know is how Paul thought of his own death as he wrote from prison:

It is my eager expectation and hope that I shall not be at all ashamed, but that with full courage now as always Christ will be honoured in my body, whether by life or by death. For to me to live is Christ, and to die is gain.

PHILIPPIANS 1:20–21

The long run

After Paul's death, the church continued to be divided
in its attitude to him between fervent supporters, fervent
opponents and the undecided. As time passed and fewer
people in his churches could remember the details of
Paul's preaching, the letters that had seemed an incidental
by-product of his mission became ever more valuable as
a concrete preservation of his teaching. Church leaders
made copies so that they could be shared around, and it
is thought that around AD 100 someone edited them into a
single volume. Alongside the four Gospels, they started to
become the new scriptures of the Christian church, giving
Paul and his teaching a central place that he never had in
his own day.

For the church leaders who wrote around the start of
the second century – Clement, Ignatius and Polycarp – Paul

The apocryphal Paul

Many writings about or supposedly by Paul appeared in the two centuries after
he died. Some were letters in his name, supporting one side or another in
theological disputes, or recreating lost letters mentioned in the Bible, such as to
Laodecia. There is a series of chummy letters between Paul and the philosopher
Seneca.

Two books purport to recount the vision of heaven which God forbade Paul
to talk about, according to 2 Corinthians 12. In one, Paul gets the better of the
Creator, who tries to stop him getting beyond the seventh heaven. The other
also contains graphic scenes of hell, after which Paul persuades God to let the
damned have Sundays off.

The long *Acts of Paul* describes his missionary exploits raising the dead,
healing the blind and preaching celibacy. He works closely with a female apostle,
Thecla, and survives being thrown to the lion in Ephesus because he had
previously converted and baptized it. When he is beheaded in Rome, milk spurts
out. (The author, a minister, was sacked for writing it.)

Paul was not every writer's hero, though, and in the *Kerygmata Petrou*,
written by conservative Jewish Christians, he is Peter's arch-enemy, a false
prophet to the Gentiles after whom Peter comes 'as healing after sickness'.

Paul at the
church of
St Paul's Outside
the Wall, Rome.

was a hero, an icon of endurance and fortitude, though only Clement shows much understanding of what Paul actually taught. Vehement opposition to Paul also continued, though, hardening in the second century into a Jewish Christian faction called the Ebionites. It probably originated in the Jerusalem church, and they looked to James and Peter as their heroes, Paul being their Antichrist.

At the other extreme, an Asia Minor convert called Marcion devoted himself to Paul to the exclusion of the rest of Christianity. He rejected not just the law of Moses, but every Jewish element of the faith, including the Jewish God, the Old Testament, all the Gospels except Luke and even many passages in Luke and Paul that

sounded too Jewish and so must have been added later. He
was expelled by the mainstream church but his rival ultra-
Pauline version of Christianity was extremely successful
during his lifetime.

Marcion's challenge compelled the church to start
trying to decide which writings would constitute its
authoritative scriptures, and, although it was a painfully
long process, the thirteen letters of Paul, along with the
four Gospels, were in there unchallenged from the start.
From this point, Paul's position at the heart of Christian
orthodoxy was assured, though it was still possible for
Justin, one of the two major authors of the second
century, to write as if Paul had never existed.

Since then an extraordinary number of controversial new movements in the history of the church have been inspired by Paul. His teaching on the value of celibacy was an impetus on the first monastic movement. The father of the Western church, Augustine, was converted by reading Paul, and took from him the theological system that was its foundation, in which fallen humanity cannot save itself and is utterly dependent on the grace of God. In the Reformation, it was Paul's teaching of justification by faith that inspired and informed Luther's revolt against medieval Catholicism. Soon afterwards, both the Reformed and Baptist traditions began on the basis of Paul's teaching about the spirituality of the new covenant. John Wesley, father of both Methodism and evangelicalism, not only saw the moment of his conversion as being when he heard someone reading Luther's preface to Romans, but also based his faith on Paul's idea of dying to the old self and living by the Spirit. Once again in the twentieth century, the great impact of Karl Barth came through his hearing and broadcasting the 'mighty voice of Paul' in Romans.

The fact that fresh readings of Paul have so often had such a radical impact on the church makes one wonder whether his natural condition is to be constantly heard and never understood, whether to grasp him properly will always mean upsetting pews. However, one also wonders how many of the people listed Paul would actually have got on with and agreed with. Perhaps his greatest tribute is not so much that he has inspired theological revolutionaries, like himself, and great religious campaigns, but that countless generations of ordinary Christians have heard his words and found in them comfort, rebuke, wisdom, inspiration, new understanding of Jesus Christ, and above all the challenge to embody in their own life, by the power of the Spirit, the death and resurrection of the messiah.

Chronology

(All except imperial dates are very approximate.)

27 BC: Accession of Augustus, first Roman Emperor.

4 BC: Most accepted date for the birth of Jesus. Paul born around the same time.

14 AD: Emperor Augustus succeeded by Tiberius.

27: Start of Jesus' mission.

30: (Passover) Crucifixion.

32: Execution of Stephen.

33: Conversion of Paul. He goes to Arabia and Damascus.

36: Emperor Tiberius succeeded by Gaius (Caligula). Paul leaves Damascus for Jerusalem and then Cilicia.

41: Emperor Gaius succeeded by Claudius. Barnabas brings Paul to Antioch.

42: Paul's missionary journey with Barnabas, to Cyprus and Galatia.

47: Circumcisers come to Antioch from Jerusalem.

48: The Jerusalem council. Paul falls out with Barnabas and Peter.

49: Missionary journey to Galatia with Silas, then with Silas and Timothy to Philippi and Thessalonica.

50: From Thessalonica to Athens and Corinth. *1 and 2 Thessalonians.*

51: Paul tried before Gallio and leaves Corinth for Antioch and then Galatia. *Galatians.*

52: Paul comes to Ephesus for three years.

54: Emperor Claudius succeeded by Nero.

55: *1 Corinthians.* Paul starts his collection for Jerusalem.

56: Disputes at Corinth. *2 Corinthians.*

57: *Romans.* Paul brings the Gentiles' offering to Jerusalem. Arrest, and imprisonment in Caesarea.

59: Paul sent from Caesarea to Rome. Shipwreck in Malta.

60: Paul arrives in Rome. Prison for at least two years.

62: Killing of James, the brother of Jesus.

64: Great fire of Rome.

65: Nero's massacre of Christians.

Suggestions for Further Reading

First-century sources

There is, of course, no substitute for reading Paul's own writings, preferably in one sitting as letters, not divided up into Bible readings. Countless translations are available. Quotations in this book are from the excellently reliable New Revised Standard Version (NRSV); the Good News Bible is a very good combination of accuracy and readability.

For the *Didache* and other first- and second-century writings, see M. Staniforth and A. Louth (eds and trs), *Early Christian Writings*, Harmondsworth: Penguin, 1987. Alternatively visit http://www.earlychristianwritings.com, which has older translations available for free and also includes the apocryphal writings I have referred to.

Reference

G.F. Hawthorne, R.P. Martin and D.G. Reid (eds), *Dictionary of Paul and his Letters*, Leicester: IVP, 1993.

Introductions

These cover both Paul's life and thought, except for Hengel who focuses on a smaller area. Bornkamm and Sanders are the more sceptical authors.

G. Bornkamm, *Paul*, Philadelphia: Fortress Press, 1995.

F.F. Bruce, *Paul: Apostle of the Free Spirit*, Exeter: Paternoster Press, 1980.

M. Hengel, *The Pre-Christian Paul*, London: SCM Press, 1991.

E.P. Sanders, *Paul: A Very Short Introduction*, Oxford: Oxford University Press, 2001; previously published as *Paul*, Past Masters Series, Oxford: Oxford University Press, 1991.

N.T. Wright, *What Saint Paul Really Said*, Oxford: Lion Hudson, 1997.

Classic scholarship

R. Bultmann, *Theology of the New Testament*, vol. 1, New York: Charles Scribner's Sons, 1951.

W.D. Davies, *Paul and Rabbinic Judaism*, Philadelphia: Fortress Press, 1980 (1948).

E. Käsemann, *Commentary on Romans*, Grand Rapids: Eerdmans, 1980 (1973).

E.P. Sanders, *Paul and Palestinian Judaism*, London: SCM Press, 1977.

A. Schweitzer, *The Mysticism of Paul the Apostle*, London: A. & C. Black, 1953 (1930).

Recent studies on Paul

James D.G. Dunn, *The Theology of Paul the Apostle*, Grand Rapids: Eerdmans, 1997.

B. Witherington, III, *The Paul Quest: The Renewed Search for the Jew of Tarsus*, Leicester: IVP, 1999.

N.T. Wright, *The Climax of the Covenant: Christ and the Law in Pauline Theology*, Philadelphia: Fortress Press, 1992.

Acts

C.K. Barrett, *Acts: A Shorter Commentary*, London: Continuum, 2002.

M. Hengel, *Acts and the History of Earliest Christianity*, London: SCM Press, 1979. (Hengel's is not an extensive commentary on Acts so much as a defence of it.)

B. Witherington, III, *The Acts of the Apostles: A Socio-Rhetorical Commentary*, Grand Rapids: Eerdmans, 1998.

Index

Picture and Text Acknowledgments

Pictures

Text

Lion Hudson

Commissioning editor: Morag Reeve

Project editor: Olwen Turchetta

Designer: Nicholas Rous

Production manager: Kylie Ord